Mary Letitia Chalmers

Our Kith and Kin

A History of the Harris Family, 1754-1895

Mary Letitia Chalmers

Our Kith and Kin
A History of the Harris Family, 1754-1895

ISBN/EAN: 9783337126643

Printed in Europe, USA, Canada, Australia, Japan

Cover: Foto ©Andreas Hilbeck / pixelio.de

More available books at **www.hansebooks.com**

Our Kith and Kin

or,

A History

of

The Harris Family

by

Mary Letitia Chalmers

1754-1895

DEDICATION.

As an affectionate tribute to my dear grandchildren, Eva, Mary Agnes, Palmer and James Cuyler Chalmers; and to the youth of the present generation of the descendants of John and Eleanor Reynolds Harris, this volume is inscribed by the author, with the fond hope that it may be in some measure instrumental in leading them to embalm in grateful and loving memory the names and virtues of their pious and noble ancestors, and to bequeath to succeeding generations a spotless name with increasing splendor.

PREFACE.

This modest little volume owes its existence to what was at first a small collection of matter for the information of the writer's immediate family. Friends desired and asked for its publication. Then other matter was obtained, hence the present form and arrangement of the book.

It is not given to the public as a complete record of all the descendants of the Harris Family, but the author's aim and desire were to make it complete, and to this end neither time, labor, nor expense were spared in the collection of material.

It may be, doubtless will be, disappointing to some, but when it is remembered that the families are scattered abroad over this South land from Virginia to Texas, that some have been lost sight of entirely, that in some instances valuable records have been lost or destroyed, while in a few instances little or no taste or interest is felt by the present generation in such matters, it is a source of gratification that so much reliable information has been gathered and arranged in a simple, intelligible and permanent form.

To all who have so kindly aided us in the collection of materials public acknowledgment is herewith most gratefully made.

If this little volume shall in any degree serve to keep green and fragrant the memory of our worthy ancestors, or contribute to the instruction and pleasure of any descendant, or stimulate and encourage a single reader to collect and preserve materials for future history, the author will feel that she has not written in vain.

M. L. C.

Charlotte, N. C., June 1, 1895.

CONTENTS.

	Page
CHAPTER I—In Bonds and Imprisonment.	5
" II—John Harris and Eleanor Reynolds.	13
" III—Hugh Harris, oldest son of John and Eleanor Harris. John Harris and Isabella Grier, children of Hugh Harris. Martha Harris Witherspoon, daughter of Isabella Grier, and her children, the Bells, Witherspoons and Boyces.	18
" IV—Rev. Robert Calvin Grier, D.D., son of Isabella Harris Grier and grandson of Hugh Harris.	28
" V—Eleanor Robison, third child of Hugh Harris, and her children, Isabella G. Grier, Martha A. Bell, Deborah E. Cannon and Hugh H. Robison.	38
" VI—Robert Harris and Hugh Harris, Jr., sons of Hugh Harris, Sr., and grandsons of John and Eleanor.	54
" VII—Jane Harris Peoples, youngest child of Hugh Harris, Sr., and her children, Hugh Harris, John Brown, Isabella Hunter, Matthew Henry, James Harvey and Richard Ramsey.	69
" VIII—Descendants of Robert Harris, second son of John and Eleanor Reynolds Harris.	82
" IX—John Harris, Jr., third son of John and Eleanor Reynolds Harris, and Mary Grier, eldest child of John Harris, Jr.	107
" X—Nancy Harris Strong, third child of John Harris, Jr., and her children, Dr. John Mason Strong, Martha Jane Young and Mary Letitia Chalmers.	114
" XI—Eleanor Euphemia Young and Nancy Caroline Patterson, youngest children of Nancy Harris Strong.	127
" XII—Dr. John Moore Harris and Martha Harris Strong, youngest children of John Harris, Jr.	138
" XIII—James Harris, fourth and youngest son of John and Eleanor Reynolds Harris.	152
CONCLUSION.	165

CHAPTER I.

IN BONDS AND IMPRISONMENT.

Our narrative begins with a marriage solemnized within the gloomy walls of a prison. We sometimes witness marriages in churches, brilliantly lighted, with elaborate decorations, large audiences and the music of the deep toned organ; sometimes in ancestral halls among friends and relations who load the happy pair with costly presents and congratulations; sometimes in the humbler walks of life with but few to witness; and occasionally a "Gretna Green" affair.

But in the case of John Harris and Eleanor Reynolds, our worthy and esteemed ancestors, how very different!

On January 23, 1754, Rev. Thomas Clark, M. D., the beloved pastor of John and Eleanor, at Ballybay congregation, Ireland, was arrested by the civil authorities, at the instigation of his Socinianized Presbyterian enemies, while in the very act of moderating in a call in the congregation of New Bliss.

The charge was disloyalty, because he refused to swear by "Kissing the Book," believing it to be unscriptural, and also because he refused to take the "Oath of Abjuration," inasmuch as it recognized the king as the head of the Church, though he had proven his loyalty by entering the army while a theological student and fighting against the Pretender.

Here is Dr. Clark's own statement of the affair:

"They well knew that the Associate Synod of Scotland, to which I belonged, scrupled at the form of 'Book Kissing,' so in hopes to drive me out of the kingdom they summoned me on the Lord's day to swear the State Oath and Kiss the Book, which I refused to do. They fined me and afterward committed me to jail."

All that night, after his arrest, he was kept under guard in a tavern, and the next day taken to Monaghan Jail.

Many of his people accompanied him, and instead of allowing them to rescue him as they would have done, they sang portions of the 18th Psalm.

> "And from above the Lord sent down
> And took me from below;
> From many waters he me drew,
> Which would me overflow.
> He me relieved of my strong foes,
> And such as did me hate;
> Because he saw that they for me
> Too strong were and too great.
>
> They me prevented in the day
> Of my calamity;
> But even then the Lord himself
> A stay was unto me.
> He to a place where liberty
> And room was, hath me brought;
> Because he took delight in me,
> He my deliverance wrought.

> The Lord will light my candle so
>   That it shall shine full bright;
> The Lord my God will also make
>   My darkness to be light.
> Who but the Lord is God? but he
>   Who is a rock and stay?
> 'Tis God that girdeth me with strength,
>   And perfect makes my way."

Such a man, like Paul, might suffer trouble as an evil doer, even unto bonds, but the word of God could not be bound.

During his imprisonment, like the great apostle to the Gentiles when a prisoner at Rome, Dr. Clark wrote frequent letters of instruction and comfort to his devoted people, who cheered and brightened the gloomy hours of their pastor's prison life by many tokens of love and loyalty. He preached to as many of them as could convene on the Sabbath, poured the baptismal waters upon the brows of thirteen little children, and married at least one couple, John Harris and Eleanor Reynolds. This last tender and beautiful act of devotion to their pastor on the part of two young lovers must have made a deep and lasting impression upon Dr. Clark, for nearly forty years afterwards he refers to it with manifest pleasure in the last document his hand ever wrote.

When the day of trial came his commitment was found to be erroneous and the whole thing a fraud and he was immediately discharged. He was urged to prosecute his persecutors with every assurance of success, but he refused, saying: "Vengence is mine; I will repay, saith the Lord."

We cannot better close this initial chapter than with a sketch of this eminent and useful man of God.

Rev. Thomas Clark, M. D., was born in Scotland, November 5, 1720.

He graduated at Glasgow University, where he took the degree of Doctor of Medicine; served his country faithfully in the army which fought against the Pretender during the years 1745-46; commenced the study of theology in the Associate Hall, and finished after the schism of 1747 in the Burgher Hall, under Ebenezer Erskine; was licensed April, 1748, by the Presbytery of Glasgow; preached about one year in Scotland and two years in Ireland; was ordained and installed pastor of the congregation of Ballybay, Ireland, July 23, 1751; was imprisoned in Monaghan Jail, January 23d to April, 1754; sailed from Newry, Ireland, for America, May 10 or 16, 1764, and landed at New York, July 28, 1764.

When ready to sail it was found that the mass of his congregation, to the extent of three hundred souls, were ready to accompany him to America.

After landing, a portion of his parishioners went to Abbeville Co., S. C., where some friends had gone before, but the great majority settled with him in Salem, N. Y. His pastoral relation had never been disturbed; his church had simply been transplanted, and he continued on in Salem as the pastor of the eight ruling elders and one hundred and fifty communicants and children that had come with him from Ballybay.

After at least three visits to South Carolina Dr. Clark resigned his charge at Salem, N. Y., and became pastor of Cedar Spring and Long Cane in Abbeville Co., S. C. in 1785, where he died of apoplexy on the 25th of December, 1792. His remains lie in the graveyard at Cedar Spring, Abbeville Co., S. C. The grave is enclosed and covered with a marble slab, bearing the following inscription, which is remarkable for its inaccuracies:

To the Memory of
Rev. Thomas Clark, D. D.
Who was born in Ireland,
Licensed to preach April, 1748,
Labored in Ballybay 16 years,
Emigrated to N. Y., 28th June, 1764,
After laboring there many years came to Abbeville,
S. C., 1786, where he labored as the founder and first
pastor of Cedar Spring and Long Cain until his death,
December 26, 1792.

There are four errors in the above inscription; Dr. Clark was an M. D., not a D. D.; he was born in Scotland, not Ireland; landed in America July 28th, not June, and died December 25th, not 26th.

Dr. Clark's Hebrew Bible is in possession of Rev. John T. Chalmers, of Philadelphia. It consists of two volumes, finely bound in calf, gilt edges, date 1667, consequently is two hundred and twenty-eight years old. Each volume bears the following autograph, in a large, clear hand: "Thomas Clark, of New Perth, in County of Charlotte in New York Colony, owner of this book. Came from Toofeehee in parish of Tannidos in the shire of Angus, in the Kingdom of Scotland, November 5th, 1720."

Just below this inscription in Dr. Clark's own handwriting is the following: "Now the book of William Blackstocks from Leggygowan, near Saintfield, in the county of Down, Ireland; bought May 23d, 1793. And he esteems it an honour, though he's sensible of his unworthiness, to have his name upon the same page with such a great and good man as he who was the former owner of this book."

Thus the volumes were owned consecutively by the two only pastors John and Eleanor Harris ever had.

We close this sketch with the following from Scouller's Manual: "Dr. Clark was a man of blunt manners and of great eccentricities of character, but he was wholly devoted to the cause of Christ and in active labors exceedingly abundant. Wherever he went and in whatever he was engaged, he preached Christ, and the Lord greatly blessed his labors. He had a marvelous ability in adapting himself to circumstances and in turning them to good. While once preaching two dogs met in front of the pulpit and began a fight. After they were ejected and quiet restored, instead of going on with his sermon he asked his people if they knew what these dogs had been doing. He said they had been preaching, and that the subject of their discourse was original sin and the consequences of the fall, and then added some illustrations and applications which they never forgot.

On one occasion, while traveling in Vermont, he

fell into company with a stranger with whom he rode a good part of the day. Coming at last to a place where their roads parted, they bade each other farewell, and rode each on his own way for a short distance. The Doctor then stopped and called to his fellow traveler to come back, that they had forgotten something.

When met again at the forks of the road the Doctor said: "Sir, we have been been traveling together some hours, enjoying each other's company, and may never meet again. I think it would be well before parting to have a word of prayer."

They dismounted, and kneeling by the roadside, the Doctor made an appropriate and fervent prayer. He then proposed to the other that he should pray. He declined to do so, and being much importuned at last acknowledged that he had never prayed in his life. The Doctor would take no denial. He told him that if he had never prayed hitherto, it was high time to begin. The man, finding that there was no escape, kneeled down and said, "Lord thou knowest that I can't pray at all." "That," said the Doctor, "is an excellent beginning; only persevere and you will do well." This was the means of the conversion of that man, who became an active and useful Christian.

Sabbath morning once found him in the tavern of a Virginia hamlet, where there was no place for religious worship; multitudes were crowding in from the surrounding neighborhood, and he soon learned that a horse race was the order of the day. He mingled with the throng, and just before the event was to come off he raised himself into an elevated position, and with a loud voice called out: "There is danger, my friends, there is danger here; let us ask God to take care of us and bless us"; and immediately commenced a prayer which produced a very general and powerful impression. Seeing his advantage he followed this with a sermon, and when that was over the crowd concluded that it was too late for the race, and dispersed.

His publications were, "Some Letters (4) from the Rev. Thomas Clark, minister of the Gospel, to his congregation at the new meeting house in Ballybay, while prisoner in Monaghan Jail," pp. 52, 1754; "Plain Reasons, a pamphlet in defence of the use of the Psalms in praise;" and a "Pastoral and Farewell Letter to the Associate Congregation in Ballybay by their Former Pastor, pp. 72, printed in Salem in 1811." This letter was unfinished; he was in the very act of writing it when he died.

He had just finished writing, "What I do thou knowest not now; but thou shalt know hereafter." Here his pen dropped from his fingers forever, for he was dead.

CHAPTER II.
JOHN HARRIS AND ELEANOR REYNOLDS.

John Harris and Eleanor Reynolds, the ancestors of the "Harris Family," whose history, together with that of their numerous descendants, it is our purpose to briefly recount in the following pages, were parishioners of Rev. Thomas Clark, M. D., and natives of Monaghan County, Ireland.

John Harris was born in 1727 and Eleanor Reynolds in 1726.

They were among the number of faithful followers who accompanied Dr. Clark to prison in January, 1754, for their youngest son, James Harris, the author of a little work on Psalmody, known as the "Plowman's Letter," says in the book: "I heard my mother mention to Dr. Clark that she remembered that on their way to jail they sang the 29th verse of the 18th Psalm (old version):

> " By thee through troops of men I break,
>   And then discomfit all:
>   And by my God assisting me,
>   I overleap a wall,"

which promises were made good to him, for he was honorably acquitted."

John and Eleanor had their marriage solemnized by Dr. Clark, during his incarceration, the latter part of January, 1754.

A few months later they sailed for America, and we may be sure the voyage was a long and tedious one, and very uncomfortable in the sail vessels of that period compared with a six days' trip at the present time in a magnificent palace steamer that almost annihilates time and space.

Their ship was detained in quarantine for a length of time, during which detention their first born saw the light. After landing they settled and remained for several years in Lancaster County, Pa. Then they moved to North Carolina and located temporarily on "Goose Creek" in either Mecklenberg or Union Counties, N. C. This removal probably took place about the year 1767 or 1768.

In a short time they secured a large tract of land, known as "Indian Land," situated partly in Mecklenburg County, N. C., and in York district, S. C. Here they found a permanent home and spent the remainder of their days.

This last settlement was likely made prior to 1775, as we learn from a history of Steele Creek by Rev. J. B. Watt that as early as 1775 a few families from Lancaster County, Pa., originally from Ireland, settled in Steele Creek, and from that time till their organization in 1792 or 1793, received supplies by ministers direct from Ireland and Pennsylvania, and among others "Clark" is named. (Rev. Thomas Clark, we presume.)

John and Eleanor Harris preceded Dr. Clark to this country by at least ten years, and "tradition" says that John Harris rode all the way from South Carolina to New York on horseback, leading an extra horse for the doctor to ride back, and that in this way he made his first visit to the South.

Dr. Robert Lathan, in his "History of the Associate Reformed Synod of the South," says that Dr. Clark visited that portion of his congregation which went to South Carolina in 1769 (page 161); that he filled appointments in Carolina between May 1, 1770, and November 6th of the same year (page 267); that in the Fall of 1779 he preached to congregations in North Carolina when on his way to visit that part of his congregation which had settled in Abbeville County, S. C. (page 269); returning North he was released from the pastoral care of Salem, N. Y., in the Spring of 1782, and repairing to South Carolina again labored there during 1782 and 1783; returned North again in 1783 and labored as missionary of the Associate Reformed Church for two years; returned South in 1785 and began to labor permanently in Abbeville County, S. C., and that a call or petition for the permanent services of Dr. Clark was sent up from the churches of Abbeville County, S. C., to the Associate Reformed Synod which met in the city of Philadelphia, Pa., May 31, 1786, and that the Synod directed that he continue to labor among them till provision be made for his regular installment. (Page 270-271).

It is evident from the above that Dr. Clark made at least *four* separate visits from New York to South Carolina, and during these visits and after his permanent settlement in South Carolina, he was a welcome visitor at the comfortable home of John and Eleanor Harris.

In his last publication, a "Pastoral Letter," written from Long Cane, Abbeville County, S. C., in 1792, to the Associate congregation in Ballybay, Ireland, and printed in Salem, N. Y., in 1811, Dr. Clark says that while imprisoned "one young couple of your number came and got their marriage solemnized in prison, viz.: John Harris and Eleanor Reynolds, now settled here by the Catawba River. She lately died an eminent Christian, and her children still act as firm friends to religion, and are in comfortable circumstances."

John Harris was born in Ireland in 1727, and died at his residence in Lower Steele Creek, or Blackstock neighborhood, June 8, 1808, aged eighty-one years.

Eleanor Reynolds Harris, his wife, was born in Ireland in 1726, and died August 22, 1789, aged sixty-three years.

Their remains repose in the churchyard at Big Steele Creek, Mecklenburg County, N. C. This was their first church home, and here they worshipped regularly until the introduction of human composition into the praise service of the church, thereby displacing the Psalms, Hymns and Spiritual Songs of the Inspired Psalter, forced them to withdraw and seek supplies of preaching from other sources.

A few years later they united with others in the organization of Lower Steele Creek Church, and Rev. William Blackstock from Ireland, was ordained and installed as their first pastor June 8, 1794, hence the origin of "Blackstock Church."

John and Eleanor Harris had four sons, Hugh, born January 7, 1755, and died August 11, 1825; Robert, born in 1756, and died September 28, 1841; John, born in 1763, and died September 26, 1824; James, born September 1, 1767, and died December 12, 1833.

The two oldest sons, Hugh and Robert, were in active service during the whole of the Revolutionary War.

Once they were captured and imprisoned in Camden, S. C., but with other prisioners effected their escape and rejoined the American Army.

John Harris, Sr., and three of his sons, Hugh, John, Jr., and James, were prominent in the organization of Lower Steele Creek or Blockstock's Church, in 1792 or 1793. James was elected and ordained one of the first ruling elders.

It would seem most natural for the choice to have fallen on Hugh, the eldest, and some claim that he was an elder, but we find no record of his name among the number at the organization of the church. It is probable however that he was an Elder in Sardis Church as early as 1808.

The descendants of this historic couple have borne an active part in perpetuating the church to the present day.

CHAPTER III.

HUGH HARRIS, OLDEST SON OF JOHN AND ELEANOR. JOHN HARRIS AND ISABELLA GRIER, CHILDREN OF HUGH HARRIS. MARTHA HARRIS WITHERSPOON, DAUGHTER OF ISABELLA GRIER, AND HER CHILDREN, THE BELLS, WITHERSPOONS AND BOYCES.

Hugh, the oldest son of John and Eleanor Reynolds Harris, was born January 7, 1755, on board the ship in which his parents sailed for America, during a protracted quarantine. At what port they landed we are not able to say. Their home was for twelve or thirteen years in Lancaster County, Pa., then they came south and permanently settled in Steele Creek, N. C. In a few years the country was involved in the "Revolutionary War," and Hugh and his brother Robert enlisted as soldiers and served through the war.

They endured many of the hardships of war, including a capture and brief imprisonment at Camden, S. C., but in the day of battle their "heads were covered," and they lived to enjoy the blessings of peace and liberty.

Hugh was married on the 11th of January, 1780, to Martha Robison, of Mecklinburg County, North Carolina. Martha was connected with that numerous family of Robisons, the early settlers of Sugar Creek, N. C. Hugh was a man much esteemed in his day, and was noted for his strict punctuality in attending the public ordinances of the church. His home was some thirteen miles distant from the church in which he worshipped two-thirds of the time, but he was usually among the first arrivals at the place Sabbath morning.

He died after a lingering sickness, as we learn from the diary of Martha Harris, his brother John's wife. "Hugh Harris, senior, departed this life upon the 11th day of August, 1825, after an illness of about ten months, which he endured with Christian patience and resignation." This diary was written seventy years ago, and is still in a good state of preservation, and contains much *reliable* information as to dates and events. Hugh died in the seventy-first year of his age.

Martha R. Harris, his wife, was born December, 1754, and died January 25, 1834, aged eighty years.

The remains of both lie in the cemetery at Big Steele Creek Church, Mecklinburg County, North Carolina.

Hugh's home was one mile east of Lower Steele Creek Church, near the public road, known then—and also at the present day, as "The Nation Ford Road," Nation Ford being on the Catawba River. The location is now known as the Burns' Place. Their children were six in number, John, Isabella, Eleanor, Robert, Hugh and Jane. John, the eldest child of Hugh and Martha R. Harris, was born in Mecklinburg County, N. C., February 6, 1781. John married Nancy Matthews, of Providence, Mecklinburg County, N. C.

Soon after their marriage they removed to Maury County, Tenn., and settled on a farm in the vicinity of Hopewell Associate Reformed Church. Here they lived and died; leaving no children. John Harris died May 13, 1859, aged seventy-eight years. Nancy Matthews Harris died January 16, 1866. Their remains lie in the cemetery at Hopewell Church, Maury County, Tenn., and while no marble designates the place of their rest, a few of the oldest residents can still point out their graves.

Isabella, second child of Hugh and Martha R. Harris, was born in Mechlinburg County, N. C., August 13, 1783.

August 3, 1808, she was married to Rev. Isaac Grier, D. D., one of the fathers of the "Associate Reformed Church South." Rev. Isaac Grier was born in Green County, Georgia, in 1776, and was the first Presbyterian minister produced by the state of Georgia. This fact is learned from the epitaph of his mother's tombstone, whose remains rest in the cemetery at Sardis Church, Mecklinburg County, N. C. It is the following:

> In memory of Margaret Grier, a native of Ireland,
> and mother of the first Presbyterian minister
> Georgia produced. Died April 3rd, 1825.
> Aged 74 years.
> "It is sown in dishonour; it is raised in glory;
> It is sown in weakness; it is raised in power."

His parents were Covenanters, or Reformed Presbyterians, and he was baptised by Rev. James Martin, an itinerant Covenanter minister, in Cabarrus County,

N. C., where his parents had taken refuge from the more dangerous hostilities of the frontier during the Revolutionary War.

His academical education was under the Revs. Cunningham and Cummins, who conducted an academy in Georgia. He graduated from Dickinson College, Carlisle, Pa., under the presidency of Dr. Nesbit, in 1800.

His theological studies were under the private instruction of Rev. Alexander Porter, pastor of Long Cane Associate Reformed Church, in Abbeville County, S. C. He received license September 2, 1802, and was ordained in 1804 by the first Presbytery of the Carolinas, at Sardis church, Mecklinburg County, N. C., and installed as pastor of that congregation in connection with Providence and Waxhaws. In 1808 he demitted Waxhaws, and was installed over Blackstocks. In 1815 he resigned Providence and gave his full time to Sardis and Blackstocks. Here he labored faithfully till declining health forced him to resign in 1842. He departed this life November 2, 1843, aged sixty-seven years. Isabella, his wife, died in 1841, aged fifty-eight years. Their remains rest in the cemetery at Sardis Church, Mecklinburg County, N. C., where Dr. Grier was pastor for thirty-seven years.

Dr. Grier and Isabella had three children—Martha Harris, Robert Calvin and Isaac. Isaac died in early childhood.

Martha Harris married Rev. John G. Witherspoon,

of the Associate Reformed Church, May, 1833. John G. Witherspoon was a son of John Witherspoon, an elder in Sardis Church, N. C. He received his collegiate education at Jefferson College, Pennsylvania, graduating in 1831. Was licensed by the first Presbytery in 1833; accepted a call from Gilead, in Mecklinburg County, and from Coddle Creek and New Perth, in Iredell County, N. C., and in 1834 was ordained and installed over these churches. He soon demitted Gilead, but retained Coddle Creek and New Perth till his death, which occurred January 6, 1846, in his thirty-fourth year. A violent attack of pneumonia settled on the brain, and he was cut off, as it were, in the morning of his days. His remains lie in the cemetery at Coddle Creek Church, N. C.

The children by this marriage were Isabella Jane, John Grier and James Meridith. Isaac Newton died February 12, 1843, aged one year.

Isabella Jane Witherspoon married Charles E. Bell, of Fairfield County, S. C., March 19, 1853. Charles E. Bell was born March 27, 1828, and died January 18, 1893. His remains lie in the cemetery at Ebenezer Church, Mecklinburg County, N. C.

The children of Isabella and Charles E. Bell are seventeen in number. John Calvin, born April 10, 1854; Charles Jefferson, born October 18, 1855, and died June 14, 1863; James Sylvanus, born April 17, 1857; Frederick Oscar, born January 27, 1859; Edward Martin, born January 17, 1861; Martha, born May 26, 1862; Eunice Grier, born April 10, 1864; Jessie

Haseltine, born January 27, 1866; Charles Boyce, born September 12, 1867; Margaret Isabella, born February 5, 1869: Lillian Livingston, born October 11, 1870; Mary Caldwell, born February 14, 1874, and died March 11, 1875; Clifford, born April 11, 1875; Charles M., born August 5, 1876; Samuel Meridith, born November 12, 1877; an infant son died June 8, 1879, aged three weeks; and Laura White, born October 13, 1880.

John Calvin, oldest child of Charles and Isabella Bell, was married to Sue Johnson, of Charlotte, N. C., November 23, 1878. Their children are nine in number—Mortimore, Johnsie, Isabella, Kate and Josie, twins; Leo, Mattie, Charles and Edward. John Calvin resides in Charlotte, N. C. He is a ruling elder in Ebenezer Church near Charlotte.

James Sylvanus, third child of Isabella and Charles Bell, graduated from Erskine College under the Presidency of Dr. W. M. Grier in 1881. He chose the medical profession, took a full course in Maryland University and graduated in 1886. He located at Matthews, Mecklinburgh County, N. C., and married Ellie Reid of Matthews, N. C., October 20, 1886. He was building up a fine practice and was an influential member of Sardis Church, when attacked with pneumonia which in a few days ended his life, November 1, 1890, in the thirty-third year of his age, leaving a widow and two daughters, Mary Isabella and Jessie Grier.

Frederick Oscar, fourth child of Charles and Isabella Bell, married Anna Neely of Steele Creek, N. C.,

October 28, 1890, a daughter of the late Starr Neely. Anna was born February 10, 1864. Their children are, Frederick Oscar, Jr., born July 30, 1891, John Witherspoon, born August 27, 1892, and Lois born November 22, 1893.

Edward Martin, fifth son of Isabella and Charles Bell, married Anna McDonald of Charlotte, N. C., July 20. 1894. Their home is in Charlotte where he is in business.

Martha, sixth child, married Christopher Strong Brice of Fairfield, S. C., September 10, 1884, a descendant of the John Harris branch. Her children will be mentioned under their father's name.

Eunice Grier, seventh child of Isabella and Charles Bell, married W. Ell Younts December 23, 1885. Their only child is Samuel and they live in Pineville, N. C.

Jesse Haseltine, eighth child of Isabella and C. E. Bell, was married at the home of her parents in Mecklinburgh County, N. C., by Rev. C. E. McDonald, October 28, 1885, to William L. McDonald, son of the late Rev. L. McDonald. William L. is a graduate of Erskine College, S. C., also of a law school in Washington, D. C. Their home is in Charlotte, N. C. They have four children, William L., Jr., born September 10, 1887; Isabella, born February 11, 1889; James Sylvanus, born January 10, 1891 and Lucille, born July 23, 1893.

Margaret Isabella, tenth child, married Walter Cuthbertson of Charlotte, May, 30, 1894.

John Grier, eldest son and second child of Rev. John G. Witherspoon and Martha H., was born October 13, 1837 and married Mary Haseltine Hawthorne October 28, 1858, a daughter of Oliver Hawthorne of Abbeville County, S. C. He entered the Confederate service and was killed in battle at Kelley's Ford, Va., November 7, 1863. His body was buried in a church cemetery near where he fell. After peace was restored a monument was erected over his grave by devoted friends. Mary Haseltine Witherspoon died April 22, 1891. Her remains lie in the cemetery at Coddle Creek Church, Iredell County, N. C.

The children of these parents were Martha Isabella and John Oliver. Martha Isabella was born August 17, 1859; she was married to T. Dalton Miller of Statesville, N. C., October 2, 1878, who was born in Iredell County, February 2, 1854.

Their children are Nannie Agnew, born November 2, 1879; Robert Oliver, born November 12, 1882; an infant, born May 26 and died May 28, 1885; Mary Euphemia, born June 26, 1886; William Clark, born May 9, 1889; Lila, born November 18, 1892 and died May 22, 1893; and Rebecca Isabella, born March 31, 1894.

John Oliver, second child of John Grier and M. Haseltine Witherspoon, was born May 26, 1862. John has been married twice, first to Cora L. Patterson, June 30, 1886. The children by this marriage are John Grier, born April 9, 1887; Paul Adams, born December 18, 1888, and Cora Lewis, born January 28,

1891. Cora L. Witherspoon died March 5, 1891. John's second marriage was to Martha L. Kerr, August 5, 1891. The children are Mary Haseltine, born May 8, 1892, and one born August 8, 1894. James Meridith, youngest son of Rev. John G. and Martha Witherspoon, was born 1845. He also entered the Confederate service, was wounded at Chancellorsville, Va., survived one week and died. He was attended by Rev. John Simpson of the Associate Reformed Church, and his remains brought home and buried in the cemetery at New Hope Church, S. C. Martha H. Witherspoon's second marriage was to Rev. James Boyce January 3, 1850. He was then pastor of the Associate Reformed Churches, New Hope, and Ebenezer or Brick Church in Fairfield County, S. C. He was a son of Samuel Boyce of Sardis Congregation, born July 13, 1808, and graduated from Jefferson College, Canonsburg, Pa., in 1829. The same year he was received as a theological student by the first Presbytery of the Synod of the South. His theological course was under the private instruction of Dr. Isaac Grier. He was licensed at a meeting of Presbytery at Hopewell, Chester County, S. C., in November, 1831. In 1832 he was ordained and installed over New Hope and the Brick Church. This pastorate continued for thirty-seven years. In 1854 the title of Doctor of Divinity was conferred on him by Erskine College, S. C., and by Jefferson College, Pennsylvania, in the summer of 1854, the latter being his Alma Mater. In 1869 he was elected Professor in the Theological Seminary at Due West, S. C., to which place he removed in December of the same year. In their pleasant home near the village of Due West they spent the remainder of their days. Martha departed this life the 5th of June, 1883. Dr. Boyce filled his position in the seminary till the close of the session in June 1889. He died at the residence of his son-in-law, Dr. Lester Hunter, near to Sardis Church, Mecklinburg County, N. C., Monday, July 29, 1889. His remains were taken to Due West and placed by the side of his companion in the village church yard. Two children were the fruit of this marriage.

Martha Caroline, born October, 1851, who married Dr. Lester W. Hunter, a descendant of the same branch with herself, whose children will be considered under their father's name, and Charles Ebenezer, who died February 12, 1863, aged seven years.

CHAPTER IV.

REV. ROBERT CALVIN GRIER, D. D., SON OF ISABELLA HARRIS GRIER AND GRANDSON OF HUGH HARRIS.

Robert Calvin, second child of Rev. Isaac and Isabella Harris Grier, was born in Mecklenburg County, N. C., March 2, 1817. In 1833, in his seventeenth year, he entered Jefferson College, Canonsburg, Pa., where he graduated under the Presidency of Dr. Matthew Brown in September, 1835. After graduating he conducted successfully "Union Academy," near Sardis Church, Mecklenburg County, N. C., for two years. He began the study of theology under the direction of his father, but completed his course at Erskine Seminary, at Due West, S. C., under the Presidency of the late Rev. E. E. Pressly, D. D. He was licensed April, 1839, by the First Presbytery of the Synod of the South. Accepting a call from Bethany and Pisgah churches near King's and Crowder's Mountains, York District, S. C., and Gaston County, N. C., he was ordained and installed in June, 1841, his father, Dr. Isaac Grier officiating with other ministers. After serving these churches for the period of seven years, he was elected in October, 1847, President of Erskine College, Due West, S. C., to succeed Dr. E. E. Pressly, who resigned on account of ill-health. He was inaugurated in the Spring of 1848. In 1858, he resigned this position, and in 1859, he was by the Synod of the South, chosen Theological Professor.

During the "Civil War" the college exercises were suspended, but when re-opened, he was again elected President, which position he filled till his death. In the thirty-sixth year of his age he received the honorary title of Doctor of Divinity from Washington College, Lexington, Va. Upon the death of the pastor of Due West Congregation (Dr. E. E. Pressly), Dr. R. C. Grier was the same year, 1860, chosen as his successor. In conjunction with the duties as President of the college and Professor of Theology, he served this large congregation. The duties which these positions necessarily demanded proved too burdensome, and in the prime of his days and in the zenith of his usefulness his life came to a close on Thursday the 30th of March, 1871, in the fifty-fifth year of his age. His remains lie in the cemetery at Due West, S. C.

Dr. Robert Calvin Grier married Barbara Brown Moffatt, August, 1840, daughter of William Moffatt, of Chester County, S. C.; she graduated from the Salem Female College, N. C. The following are their children, eleven in number: Isaac Livingston, William Moffatt, Eugene, who died in infancy, July 3, 1845; Margaret Isabella, Laura Elizabeth, Martha Lois, Jane E., an infant son who died July 20, 1858, Boyce Hemphill, Paul Livingston, and Mark Brown. Isaac Livingston, eldest child of Robert Calvin Grier, was born August 28, 1841. He entered the Confederate Service and was killed in battle near Richmond, Va.,

June 27, 1862. He was a youth of much promise, and had just entered upon a course of study in the Seminary preparatory to entering the gospel ministry.

William Moffatt, second child of Robert Calvin and Barbara Grier, was born February 11, 1843, graduated in Erskine College under the presidency of his father in July, 1860, entered the Confederate service and lost a leg at the battle of Williamsburg, Va., May 5, 1862. He graduated from the Theological Seminary, Due West, S. C., in 1866. William Moffatt was licensed by the Second Presbytery April, 1866. Accepting a call from Bethel congregation, Allenton, Ala., he was ordained and installed pastor of that church August, 1867. From that pastoral charge he was elected by the "Synod of the South" at a meeting at Long Cane, Abbeville County, S. C., in September, 1871, to succeed his lamented father in the presidency of Erskine College, which position he has filled to the present time. He is also Professor in the Theological Seminary located at Due West, and principal editor of the *Associate Reformed Presbyterian*, the organ of the "Synod of the South."

He received the title of D. D. from Monmouth College, Ill., in 1872, in the twenty-ninth year of his age.

He married **Nannie** McMorris, of Newberry County, S. C., October 25, 1864. Their children, seven in number, are Jennie G., Robert Livingston, Laura E., born March 17, 1872; William Moffatt, Jr., born August 19, 1874; Helen Pauline, born December

7, 1876; Ralph Erskine, born December 8, 1881, and Agnes Hemphill, born December 1, 1884.

Jennie G., first child of Dr. William M. and Nannie Grier, was born September 2, 1865. She graduated from the Due West Female College in the class of 1883, and was married to Rev. James Strong Moffatt November 23, 1886, a son of Rev. Wm. S. Moffatt, of the Associate Reformed Church, and first A. R. minister born in Ark. Rev. J. S. Moffatt was born July 17, 1860, graduated from Muskingum College, Ohio, June 28, 1883, under the Presidency of Rev. F. M. Spencer, D. D., and from Allegheny Theological Seminary of the United Presbyterian Church March 31, 1886, under the Presidency of the late Rev. David R. Kerr, D. D., LL.D. He was licensed by the United Presbyterian Church on April 28, 1885, at Greenwoood, Mo. Being transferred from the United Presbyterian Church to the Associate Reformed Church, he was ordained by the First Presbytery June 24, 1886, at Charlotte, N. C.

James S. Moffatt supplied the church at Charlotte, N. C., for a year, and accepting a call from Chester, S. C., was installed over that church by the First Presbytery April —, 1887. The children of James and Jennie Moffatt are Julia McMorris, born March 20, 1889; James Strong, Jr., born July 17, 1891, and William Grier, born May 6, 1893.

Robert Livingston, second child of Dr. Wm. M. Grier, was born September 15, 1867. He graduated from Erskine College, Due West, S. C., June, 1887, under the Presidency of his father, Dr. W. M. Grier.

In 1891 he entered the Theological Seminary, completing his course in 1893, He was licensed at Kings Creek Church, Newberry, County, S. C., by the Second Presbytery of the Synod of the South, April, 1893. Accepting a call from Steele Creek congregation, Mecklinburg County, N. C., he was ordained and installed over that congregation by a committee of the First Presbytery, his father, Dr. Grier, of the Second Presbytery, being present and participating. It is worthy of remark that Rev. Isaac Grier, D. D., the great-grand-father of the newly installed pastor, eighty-six years ago, sustained the same relation to the ancestors of some of the members of the congregation.

Robert Livy was married May 20, 1891, to Fannie Grist, daughter of Captain L. M. Grist, Editor and Proprietor of the *Yorkville Enquirer*, and a ruling elder in the Associate Reformed Presbyterian Church, at Yorkville, S. C. Just as he was entering upon the duties of pastor and about to occupy the handsome parsonage on the church lot recently re-fitted for his reception, his wife was suddenly taken from him on June 5, 1893, and laid in the grave together with her infant. They both repose in the cemetery at Yorkville, S. C. On February 20, 1895, Rev. Robert Livy Grier was married to Jennie Marshall, of Rock Hill, S. C., a daughter of Captain J. W. Marshall, the ceremony being performed by Rev. G. T. Harmon, of the Methodist Episcopal Church.

Margaret Isabella, fourth child of Robert Calvin and Barbara Grier, was born April 5, 1847. She graduated from the Due West Female College in the class of 1862. For several years she was engaged as teacher in the college where she graduated. She was married to John E. Martin, at the residence of her father in Due West, October 27, 1864.

J. E. Martin was born in Fairfield County, S. C., March 19, 1843. He graduated from Erskine College, Due West, S. C., in 1861, under Drs. Grier and Patton. In 1867, he entered the Theological Seminary, at Due West, and graduated in 1869. The same year he was licensed by the Second Presbytery of "The Synod of the South." Accepting a call from Hopewell congregation, Newton County, Ga., he was ordained and installed by the Second Presbytery, pastor of that church in the autumn of 1871. On account of feeble health he resigned his charge in 1890. They reside near Covington, in Newton County, Ga.

Rev. John E. and M. Isabella Martin have seven children, Mary Lois, Robert Calvin Grier, Fannie Moffatt, Alice Bell, John Edward-Gary, Laura Harris and Lizzie Pauline.

Mary Lois, eldest child, graduated from the Female College, Due West, in 1885, was married to Rev. Robert Young Mills, at the residence of her parents, Newton County, Ga., September 20, 1888. R. Y. Mills is a son of Major Edward Mills of Chester County, S. C., and was born June 20, 1861. He graduated from Erskine College in 1883. After a full course in the Theological Seminary at Due West, he was licensed April 11, 1885. Accepting a call from Lancaster Church, S. C., he was installed by the First Presbytery pastor of that church November 15, 1888. His pleasant relations with this church continued only four months, for he died after a few hours sickness of congestion on March 4, 1889. His remains were conveyed to the home of his youth and interred at Hopewell, Chester County, S. C. Mary Lois returned to the home of her parents.

Fannie Moffatt, third child of Margaret Isabella and Rev. John E. Martin, married F. J. Cooledge of Atlanta, Ga., October 20, 1892.

Laura Elizabeth, fifth child of Rev Robert Calvin and Barbara Grier, was born October 12, 1849, graduated in the Due West Female College in 1867, and was married to Rev. G. R. White at the home of her mother in Due West, September 18, 1873. Mr. White is a son of the late Col. J. P. White, elder in New Sterling congregation, Iredell County, N. C. He graduated from Erskine College in 1871. His theological course was taken in the Seminary at Due West, S. C. He was licensed and ordained by the First Presbytery of "The Synod of the South;" and accepting a call from Ebenezer congregation, Mecklinburg County, N. C., was installed in 1876 pastor by the First Presbytery. His labors have continued in this field to the present time and they live in a beautiful home near to the church.

Martha Lois, sixth child of Rev. Robert C. and Barbara Grier, was born April 13, 1852. She graduated in the Due West Female College in the class of 1868, and was married to Rev. David B. Pressly at the residence of her mother in Due West, S. C., October 24, 1872. Mr. Pressly was a son of the late Rev. James P. Pressly, D. D., Professsor in Erskine College and the Theological Seminary at Due West, S. C. He graduated from Erskine College in 1869 and from the Theological Seminary at Due West in 1871 and was licensed by the Second Presbytery of the Associate Reformed Synod at King's Creek Church, Newberry County, S. C., August 11, 1871. In 1872 he accepted calls from Hinkston and Mt. Olivet churches in Kentucky, and was installed pastor of these churches in the autumn of 1872. He resigned the pastorate of these churches in 1886, and removed to Missouri where he supplied the church of Mt. Zion, Lincoln County, until his death, September 24, 1888. His remains were brought to Due West and placed in the cemetery there. Martha Lois returned to Due West and makes her home with her mother. The children of this marriage are James Grier, born December 12, 1873; Mary Young, born April 3, 1878; David Livingston, born March 25, 1881; died February 25, 1892, in his eleventh year, and an infant son who died February 12, 1883.

Jane E. H., seventh child of Rev. R. C. and Barbara Grier, was born March 15, 1855. Graduated in 1872 from the Due West Female College, and was married at the residence of her mother in Due West, September 16, 1874, to James E. Todd of Due West. She died at her home near Due West, July 14, 1884, and is buried in the cemetery at Due West. She left two children, Eunice McClintock, born, August 23,

1875, and Robert Calvin Grier, born July 20, 1877. The eldest child, Eunice McClintock, graduated from the Due West Female College, June, 1893.

An infant son, and eighth child of Rev. R. C. and Barbara Grier, died July 20, 1858.

Boyce Hemphill, ninth child of Rev. R. C. and Barbara Grier, was born at Due West, November 8, 1861. He graduated from Erskine College, Due West, S. C., June, 1882, and from the Theological Seminary at Due West, May, 1887, was licensed by the Second Presbytery at Bethel, Laurens County, S. C., April 18, 1886, and ordained at Due West, November, 1887.

For some months his labors were confined to the churches in Kentucky. In September, 1888, immediately after the death of Rev. David B. Pressly, he took charge of the Mount Zion Church, Lincoln County, Mo., and was installed pastor, October 5, 1889, by the Kentucky Presbytery. He was released from Mount Zion, May 20, 1894. Accepting calls from the churches in York County, S. C., Tirzah and Yorkville, he was installed by the First Presbytery over Tirzah, August 10, 1894, and over Yorkville, August 17, 1894.

Rev. Boyce H. Grier was married to Julia Kennedy, daughter of Professor J. P. Kennedy, of Due West, November 5, 1889. Julia died in the Hospital in St. Louis, Mo., June 3, 1890. His second marriage was to Susie M. Lee, July 28, 1891, daughter of Professor Joseph Lee of Due West. Susie M. Lee is a graduate of the Due West Female College of the class of 1887. They have one child, Joseph Lee, born October 6, 1893.

Paul Livingston, tenth child of Rev. R. C. and Barbara Grier, was born, April 28, 1864, and graduated from Erskine College, June, 1884. He was elected Professor of Mathematics in Erskine College in 1888. He married Effie L. Presby at her father's residence in Due West, December 24, 1885, the only daughter of Dr. William L. Pressly, President of the Theological Seminary of the Associate Reformed Church at Due West. Effie L. is a graduate of the Due West Female College of the class of 1880. Their children are William Pressly, born, December 26, 1887 and Robert Calvin Grier, born, October 12, 1889.

Mark Brown, eleventh and youngest child of Rev. R. C. and Barbara Grier, was born at Due West, January 3, 1867. He graduated from Erskine College, June, 1885. He graduated from the Princeton Theological Seminary, May, 1891. Imbued with a foreign missionary spirit he offered himself as a candidate for China and connected with the General Assembly Presbyterian Church, South. After completing a course in a medical college in New York City in June, 1892, he left his native land the 15th of September to engage in missionary work in China.

CHAPTER V.

ELEANOR ROBISON, THIRD CHILD OF HUGH HARRIS, AND HER CHILDREN, ISABELLA G. GRIER, MARTHA A. BELL, DEBORAH E. CANNON AND HUGH H. ROBISON.

Eleanor, third child of Hugh and Martha R. Harris, was born in Mecklinburg County, N. C., August 2, 1786, and married Ezekiel Robison of Sugar Creek, Mecklinburg, N. C., in the year 1810, and died June 8, 1854. Ezekiel Robison was born October 10, 1782, and died August 13, 1826, aged forty-four years. He was a ruling elder in Sugar Creek Presbyterian Church. His remains lie in the cemetery of that church. Eleanor was the mother of seven children,—Isabella Grier, Martha A., Deborah Eliza, Sarah A., who died September 14, 1841, in the nineteenth year of her age, Robert L., who died in childhood in 1820, James, who also died in childhood in 1827, and Hugh Harris.

Isabella Grier, first child of Eleanor Robison, was born in 1812. On March 1, 1832, married Isaac Grier, nephew of Rev. Isaac Grier, D. D. Isaac Grier died May 9, 1862, in the sixty-first year of his age. Isabella died in 1889 in the seventy-seventh year of her age. Their remains lie in the cemetery of Back Creek, Associate Reformed Church, of which church they were members. Isabella Grier was the mother of seven sons, Robert Leroy, Isaac Harris, James Robinson, Aaron, William Baxter, James Melville and John Owens.

Robert Leroy, first child of Isaac and Isabella Grier, graduated in Erskine College, August 8, 1855. April 24, 1856, he married Martha Ann Kirkpatrick, daughter of Hugh Kirkpatrick of Sardis Church. After completing his theological course he was licensed by the First Presbytery of the Synod of the South, April, 1858. Was ordained and installed pastor of the Associate Reformed Church of Troy, Obion County, Tennessee, November 19, 1860. In 1869 he demitted this pastoral charge and moved to Marshall County, Mississippi, and ministered to Mount Carmel Church and Beulah in Shelby County, Tenn. He was installed over these churches in 1872. His companion in life died June 27, 1871, and her remains lie at Mount Carmel Church. October 10, 1872, he was married the second time to Eleanor Jane Moffatt of Marshall County, Miss., daughter of the late Samuel Moffatt. In 1880 he removed to Shelby County, Tenn. Soon disease attacked him in the form at first of jaundice, which soon assumed a more serious form, resulting in death on the 16th of February, 1881. His body rests in the cemetery at Beulah Church, Tenn. He was in his forty-ninth year. His wife, Eleanor Jane, afterwards married the late Rev. David Pressly, D. D., of the Associate Reformed Church.

His children were six in number, all by the first marriage. After their mother's death they were all brought to Mecklenburg County, N. C., where they were cared for by their grandparents and reared to maturity. Their names are as follows: Isaac Oscar, Lula Isabella, Hugh Kirkpatrick, Robert Baxter, Margaret Anna and John Stewart.

Isaac Oscar, was born March 2, 1857, and died May 31, 1881. After completing his literary course he made choice of the medical profession, and entered upon his studies with zeal and energy, and was just completing the last year of the course, with a high stand in his class and bright prospects before him when his health failed. His studies were dropped in search of health, but to no avail; he lingered and died in the springtime of his life.

Lula Isabella, born March 22, 1859, married J. Walker Griffith, December 10, 1874. Her children, six in number, are Aaron Henderson, born August 14, 1875; Martha Ann, born January 21, 1882; Lizzie Gary, born December 20, 1882; Janie Kirkpatrick, born September 2, 1886, and died October 1, 1886; Oscar, born May 16, 1888, and Gertrude, born June 29, 1892.

Hugh Kirkpatrick, third child of Rev. Leroy Grier, was born September 28, 1861, and died December 5, 1881. These brothers, Oscar and Hugh, were not long separated by death. They died of the same disease (consumption), and their bodies lie side by side in the cemetery at Ebenezer Church, Mecklenburg County, N. C.

Robert Baxter, fourth child of Rev. Leroy and

Martha A. Grier, was born January 18, 1864, removed to Texas, married Lucinda E. Powell, and their children are Martha and Mildred.

Margaret A., fifth child, was born August 29, 1866. Married Thomas Harvey Stanford, October 9, 1889. They have two children, Macie and Henry.

John Stewart, youngest child of Rev. Leroy and Martha Grier, was born September 19, 1868. He graduated from Erskine College in 1891. After a full course in the Seminary of the Associate Reformed Church, at Due West, he was licensed at a meeting of the First Presbytery in Charlotte, N. C., April, 1893. Accepting a call from Ebenezer Church, Jefferson County, Ga., he was ordained and installed over that church in August, 1893.

Isaac Harris, second child of Isaac and Isabella Grier, was born August 21, 1834, married Margaret S. Parks, October 21, 1858, who died February, 1866. Three children were born to them, Margaret Isabella, born January 22, 1860; Elizabeth Jane, born December 2, 1861; and Isaac Baxter, born December 27, 1863.

Margaret Isabella, married Chalmers Furr, October 25, 1882. Her children are, Margaret Lucilla, died February 11, 1885; William Monroe, died February 22, 1890; Baxter Grier, born May 30, 1888; and Oscar Harris, born July 14, 1891.

Elizabeth Jane, married Charles E. Frazier, December 20, 1888, and her children are, Ola Bell, born 1890, and Mary Parks, born 1892.

James Robison, son of Isaac and Isabella Grier, was born July 23, 1838, and died September 19, 1838. Aaron, was born June 4, 1839, and died July 27, 1839.

William Baxter, born July 24, 1840, died November 17, 1859, while pursuing a course of study in Erskine College. He was stricken with typhoid fever during vacation, and died in the parental home; and his remains lie in the cemetery at Back Creek Church, Mecklinburg County, N. C.

James Melville, sixth son of Isaac and Isabella Grier, born September 1, 1843, married Agnes Margaretta McLaughlin, daughter of Rev. I. G. McLaughlin, pastor of Back Creek Church, March 1, 1866. Their children, ten in number, are Robert Isaac, born June 17, 1867; John Julius, born December 18, 1868; William Baxter, born August 23, 1870, died October 14, 1875; Samuel Robison, born July 25, 1872; Margaret Alice, born September 17, 1874; Anna Isabella, born August 11, 1877; Alford Livingston, born September 6, 1879; Franklin Parks, born September 17, 1881; Calvin, born April 5, 1884, and Macie Dixon, born February 25, 1886.

John Julius, second son of J. Melville and Agnes Grier, graduated in Erskine College, in 1891, and after a full course of theology in the Associate Reformed Seminary at Due West, was licensed by the Second Presbytery at King's Creek Church, Newberry County, S. C., April 1894. Accepting a call from Abbeville Church, Abbeville County, S. C., he was ordained and installed over that church by the Second Presbytery of the "Synod of the South," July 25, 1894.

John Owen, youngest son of Isaac and Isabella Grier, was born June 21, 1846, and married Mary Alice Hunter, October 19, 1869. Their children, eleven in number, are Robert Livingston, born August 28, 1870; Hugh Harris, born September 26, 1872; Josiah Williamson, born August 1, 1875; Melville Ezekiel, born September 13, 1877; Ralph Erskine, February 1, 1879; Owan Moffatt, born January 13, 1881; William Pressly, born February 28, 1883; Mary Isabella, born December 28, 1885; Lila, born August 28, 1887; Essie, born October 4, 1890; and Boyce McLaughlin, born August 9, 1894. The mother of these children died suddenly December 21, 1894.

Martha A., second child of Eleanor and Ezekiel Robison was born November 29, 1815; married Andrew Bell, of Cabarrus County, N. C., February 7, 1839, who was born January 1, 1815. Andrew and Martha Bell lived and died in the bounds of Coddle Creek Church, and their remains lie in the cemetery at that church. Andrew Bell died August 26, 1884, and Martha A. Bell died July 10, 1875. The fruit of this marriage was six children—Walter Monroe, Reetha, E. Lemuel, James De Kalb, Hannah Isabella and Jane Eliza.

Walter Monroe, first child of Andrew and Martha Bell, was born in Cabarrus County, N. C., November 12, 1839. Was married to Bettie Parks in 1865. The fruit of this union was two sons—Hugh Parks and

Andrew Ebenezer. The mother of these sons died in 1869, aged twenty-seven years. The father died May 9, 1873, aged thirty-four years. Their remains lie in the cemetery at Coddle Creek, Iredell County, N. C.

Hugh Parks, the eldest son of these parents, makes his home in Texas. Andrew Ebenezer graduated in Erskine College in 1891, and is now a student of medicine in Maryland University, Baltimore.

Eleanor Reetha, second child of Martha A. and Andrew Bell, was born December 13, 1840. Died June 27, 1848.

Ezekiel Lemuel, third child and second son of Andrew and Martha Bell, was born Jan. 18, 1844, and was married to Josephine Johnson. They have five children —William Preston, Daniel Harris, Martha Jane, Cyrus, born March 17, 1878; and Mary G., born April 15, 1882.

William Preston, eldest child of E. Lemuel and Josephine Bell, was born in Cabarras County, N. C., June 5, 1869, and was married August 4, 1891, to Frances Andrew, of Texas. They have one child, Phyde, born August 8, 1893.

Daniel Harris, second child of E. Lemuel and Josephine Belle, was born in Cabarrus County, N. C., July 11, 1872, and was married to Omega Spikes, of Texas, October 15, 1893.

Martha Jane, third child of E. Lemuel and Josephine Bell, was born in Cabarrus County, N. C., June 2, 1876, was married April 19, 1893, to Thomas J. Cawood, of Texas. Ezekiel L. Bell removed to Texas from Coddle Creek, N. C., in 1882. Their home at present is in Corsicanna, Navarro County, where he holds a public office.

James De Kalb, third son and fourth child of Martha and Andrew Bell, was born in Cabarrus County, N. C., July 5, 1846, and married Leala Patterson, of North Carolina. One child is the fruit of this marriage—Monroe Patterson. James De Kalb died September 19, 1884. His body rests in the cemetery at Coddle Creek.

Hannah Isabella, fifth child of Martha and Andrew Bell, was born in Cabarrus County, N. C., September 12, 1850. She was married to R. S. Sloan of North Carolina. They removed to Richland, Texas, and R. S. Sloan is a ruling elder in the Associate Reformed Church in Richland County, Rev. Wm. L. Patterson, pastor. These parents had seven children, only four of whom survive, viz: Harris Robison, Frank Erskine, James DeKalb, and Florence.

Jane Eliza Bell, youngest child of Martha and Andrew Bell, was born June 23, 1854, and died April 18, 1879, in the twenty-fifth year of her age, of consumption. Her remains rest in the cemetery at Coddle Creek.

Deborah Eliza, third child of Eleanor and Ezekiel Robison, was married to John Maxwell Cannon, of Cabarrus County, N. C., of the General Assembly Presbyterian Church, in the Spring of 1846. Deborah Eliza died November 10, 1852. Her remains were laid to rest in the cemetery at Coddle Creek, Iredell County, N. C. John Maxwell Cannon, died July 12,

1890, at the residence of his son-in-law, R. B. Hunter, at Huntersville, N. C. His remains lie at Coddle Creek by the side of his wife. These parents had four children, viz.: Margaret Eleanor, James Harris, John Franklin and Anna Eliza.

Margaret Eleanor, first child of Deborah, E. and J. Maxwell Cannon, was born February 28, 1847, was married October 8, 1867, to Richard Brown Hunter, son of the late Rev. John Hunter, of the Associate Reformed Presbyterian Church. Her children are given under their father's name. James Harris, second child of Deborah E. and J. Maxwell Cannon, was born December 10, 1848, and died August 1, 1866, in the eighteenth year of his age.

John Franklin, third child of Deborah E. and John Maxwell Cannon, was born January 3, 1851, and graduated from Davidson College, Mecklinburg County, N. C., June, 1869, Dr. McPhail, President. He spent the following year in study at the University of Virginia; graduated from Union Theological Seminary, Hampden Sydney, Va., May, 1873; was licensed by the Mecklinburg Presbytery at Charlotte, N. C., May 20, 1873, and immediately transferred to the care of Chesapeake Presbytery of Virginia, to take charge of the Presbyterian Church at Leesburg, Va., and was ordained and installed pastor of the Leesburg Church by the Chesapeake Presbytery, October 29, 1873. In a few years Rev. John F. Cannon resigned his charge at Leesburg, and accepted a call to the Presbyterian Church in Shelbyville, Tenn., and was installed pastor of the Shelbyville Church, May 29, 1881. His present field of labor is in St. Louis, Mo., as pastor of the Grand Avenue Church. He was installed pastor January 6, 1889. The degree of D. D. was conferred on Rev. John F. Cannon, perhaps in the year 1888. He married Mary H. Lupton, daughter of Rev. J. W. Lupton, D. D., of Clarksville, Tenn., February 24, 1880. The fruit of this marriage is three children, Julia, born December 25, 1880; John Franklin, Jr., born March 26, 1883; and Mary Lupton, born September 30, 1884.

Anna Eliza, fourth child of Deborah E. and John Maxwell Cannon, was born October 24, 1852. Anna Eliza was only a few days old at the death of her mother. She was taken to the home of her aunt, Isabella Grier, and by her reared to womanhood. She was married at the home of her brother-in-law, R. B. Hunter, Esq., by Rev. R. Z. Johnson to Elam Augustus Sample, D. D. S., October 28, 1875, son of Robert Sample. Mr. Sample was born December 25, 1843, in Hopewell, Mecklinburg County, N. C. He graduated at the Baltimore Dental College in 1870. After practising his profession for eleven years he entered the Presbyterian Seminary at Columbia, South Carolina, in 1881. After a full course in the seminary he was licensed by the Mecklinburg Presbytery at Paw Creek, North Carolina, March, 1885. In June, 1885, he was called to take charge of Franklin and Morrison Churches in Macon County, N. C. In August the same year he was ordained as evangelist by the Mecklinburg Presbytery. He labored in these churches till March, 1889, when he took charge of a group of churches in Gaston County, N. C., composed of King's Mountain, Long Creek, Hephsibah and Shiloh. In this field he labored until August, 1892, when he was called to his present field of labor in Hendersonville and Mills River Churches, N. C.

These parents, Anna Eliza and Rev. E. A. Sample, have eight children, viz: Claudia Lee, born September 10, 1876; Maggie Elnora, born August 13, 1878; Emma Jane, born June 5, 1881; Mary Elizabeth, born May 10, 1883; Mattie Bell, born April 1, 1885; Robert Cannon, born February 19, 1887; Annie Hood, born October 1, 1889, and Grace Reynolds, born December 4, 1892.

Hugh Harris, youngest child of Eleanor and Ezekiel Robison, was born in Mecklinburg County, N. C., in the bounds of Sugar Creek Church (Presbyterian), March 1, 1824. His father being a ruling elder in that church he was baptized by the pastor, Rev. Samuel Caldwell. After the death of his father in 1826 his mother returned to her mother in Steele Creek that she might take charge of her in her declining years. After the death of her mother, which took place in 1834, Eleanor removed to the bounds of Coddle Creek Church, Iredell County, N. C., where Hugh Harris connected with the Associate Reformed Church under the ministry of Rev. John G. Witherspoon.

He entered Erskine College, Due West, S. C.,

in 1844, and graduated September 15, 1847, under the Presidency of Rev. E. E. Pressly, D. D. He was taken under the care of the First Presbytery of the Associate Reformed Church, and delivered his first trial at Back Creek, Mecklinburg County, N. C.

April 18, 1848, he completed his theological studies in the Associate Reformed Seminary at Due West, S. C.; was licensed by the First Presbytery at a meeting held at old Providence Church, Augusta County, Va., September 4, 1849. After missionating for two years among the vacant churches in the bounds of Synod, he was ordained by the Alabama Presbytery in the spring of 1852, and in July 24 of the same year was installed pastor of Ebenezer Church in Tippah County, Miss., by Rev. James L. Young. He was also installed pastor of Shiloh Church in Lafayette County, Miss., the same year. This latter church he demitted October 6, 1856, at Hopewell, Pontatoc County, Miss., and devoted his whole time to Ebenezer.

During the late war he served as chaplain for nearly a year in the "Third Regiment of Mississippi Volunteers." He endured many exposures with the regiment and at the fall of Fort Donaldson, February 16, 1862, was taken prisoner and incarcerated at Johnson Island. From fearful exposure in prison life in that rigorous climate he suffered a protracted spell of sickness which brought him apparently to the gates of death. As soon as a parole could be procured, Rev. Neill M. Gordon, of Jessamine County, Ky., removed him from prison July 10, 1862, in a reduced condition of health, to his home where he tenderly nursed him until he was able to pursue his journey.

He reached his home in Tippah County, Miss., September 27, 1862. For months after his return he was on crutches and unable to stand to preach, but preached to his people in a sitting posture. These afflictions only endeared him to his people. He continued his labors with this congregation until on Thursday morning, May 19, 1881, he breathed his last. Five days before whilst visiting the sick in his congregation he was thrown from his horse and received such serious injuries that they resulted in death. His remains lie in the cemetery at Ebenezer Church, Mississippi by the side of his mother who died suddenly at his home while on a visit in 1854.

Hugh Harris Robison was married to M. Adaline Ellis, near Due West, South Carolina, October 21, 1851, by the late Rev. E. E. Pressly, D. D. She was a daughter of John Ellis, a ruling elder in the Due West congregation. The fruit of this marriage was eight children. John Ellis, Ralph Erskine, Ella Mahaly, Jane Eliza, Margaret Isabella, Hugh Harris, James Lee and Robert Melville.

John Ellis, eldest child of Rev. Hugh Harris and Adaline Robison, was born in Tippah County, Miss., July, 19, 1852. After completing his literary course in the best schools of the county John Ellis, chose the medical profession, spent the winter of 1873-4 in Jefferson Medical College Philadelphia. Graduated from the Medical College, Louisville, Ky., in 1876, and is located in Lee County, Miss., where he is practicing his profession. He is a ruling elder in Bethany Church, Rev. Samuel A. Agnew, D. D., pastor. He married Mary Ada Hawthorne January 11, 1877, daughter of the late Thomas Hawthorne of South Carolina. She was born in South Carolina, October 31, 1856. These parents have two children, Mary Adaline, born February 10, 1878, and Hugh Hawthorne, October 25, 1883.

Ralph Erskine, second child of Hugh Harris and Adaline Robison, was born in Tippah County, Miss., November 23, 1853; graduated from Erskine College, Due West, S. C., July, 1878, and has since devoted himself to teaching. He is now Principal of the High School at Salem Church, Rev. T. G. Boyce, pastor, Tipton County, Tenn. Ralph Erskine was married to Lena Douglas, at the home of her parents in New Albany, Miss., August 23, 1888, the only child of J. W. Douglas, M. D., now of Tampa, Fla. She was born January 13, 1868. The fruit of this marriage is five children, viz.: Mattie Adaline, born July 25, 1889, died August 18, 1890; John Douglas, born January 29, 1891; Hugh Harris, born October 30, 1892; David Melville and Lee Erskine, twins, born August 24, 1894.

Ella Mahaly, third child of Hugh Harris and Adaline Robison, was born in Tippah County, Miss., in 1855. She married Rev. David W. Wiseman early in 1880. They had one child, Catharine Adeline. Mr. Wiseman graduated from Erskine College, Due West, S. C., July, 1879. After a regular course in theology in the Associate Reformed Seminary at Due West he was licensed by the Memphis Presbytery in the Spring of 1881. In the Fall of 1881 a call was regularly prepared for his acceptance from Ebenezer congregation, the church so lately made vacant by the death of Rev. Hugh Harris Robison, his father-in-law. But soon David W. Wiseman was prostrated with typhoid fever and died December 22, 1881. Consequently he was never ordained and installed pastor. His remains lie in the cemetery at Ebenezer Church, Tippah County, Miss.

Ella Wiseman's second marriage was to Mr. Newton, of Union County, Miss. She was married on the afternoon of Tuesday, the 5th of March, 1895, at her mother's residence near Atoka, Tenn., by Rev. T. G. Boyce, pastor of Salem congregation.

Jane Eliza, fourth child of Hugh Harris and Adaline Robison, was born in Tippah County, Miss., February 1, 1858. Was married to W. E. Patterson, of Tippah County, Miss., January 23, 1879. W. E. Patterson was born June 23, 1852. He is a ruling elder in Ebenezer Church, Miss., Rev. James Baird, pastor. Their children, eight in number, are Effie Adaline, born November 8, 1879; Sarah Isabella, born November 23, 1880; Hugh Henderson, born March 26, 1882; Martha Ella, May 31, 1884; Ola Jane, April 15, 1886; Lena, October 8, 1888; Robert Erskine, May 1, 1891, and John Luther, August 30, 1893.

Margaret Isabella, fifth child of Rev. H. H. and Adaline Robison, was born in Mississippi January 5, 1860.; was married to Hugh Bonner Wiseman, October

30, 1882, who was born January 6, 1860. He holds the office of deacon in Ebenezer Church, Rev. J. Baird pastor. The fruit of this union is six children. Sarah Adaline, born October 31, 1883; Cora Ella, born June 8, 1885, and died October, 21, 1890; Hunter Robison, born January 7, 1888; Jennie May, born February 23, 1890, and died June 29, 1891; Anna Isabella, born May 29, 1892, and William Ralph, born June 22, 1894.

Hugh Harris, sixth child of Rev. H. H. and Adaline Robison, was born in Tippah County, Miss.; graduated from Erskine College, Due West, S. C., in the class of 1888, and was associated with his brother, Ralph E., in the Salem High School, Tennessee, but has recently accepted a professorship in Bolton College, Tenn. He was married in 1893 to Ida Wiley, of Tipton County, Tenn.

James Lee, seventh child of Rev. Hugh H. and Adaline Robison was married to Ida McCain, at the home of her parents in Idaville, Tipton County, Tenn., January 16, 1895, by Rev. T. G. Boyce, pastor of Salem congregation. This couple, so recently united in marriage, in the short period of five weeks was separated by death. James Lee died of pneumonia at his boarding house in Randolph, Tenn., (where he was engaged in the lumber business), on Friday, February 22, 1895, in the twenty-eighth year of his age. His remains rest in the cemetery of Salem Church, Tenn.

Robert Melville, eighth child of Rev. Hugh H. and Adaline Robison, is a resident of Randolph, Tenn., and was associated with James Lee in business.

CHAPTER VI.

ROBERT HARRIS AND HUGH HARRIS, JR., SONS OF HUGH HARRIS, SR., AND GRANDSONS OF JOHN AND ELEANOR.

Robert Harris, fourth child of Hugh and Martha R. Harris, was born in Mecklinburg County, N. C., December 28, 1788. He was married to Hannah Rhea, of Providence, N. C., in the year 1811 or 1812. They removed to Morgan County, Ala., near to Somerville. There they lived and died. Hannah Harris died in 1858. Robert Harris died at the residence of his son John, in Somerville, Ala., September 15, 1860, in the seventy-second year of his age. The remains of both rest in Morgan County, perhaps in the cemetery of Somerville.

The family "Record" was lost or destroyed with other valuables during the late war, consequently we are not able to give many dates respecting Robert's family.

Robert and Hannah Harris had eight children, John, Isabella, Martha, James Leroy, Sarah Elizabeth, Amanda, Cynthia Witherspoon, and William Robert.

John, the eldest child of Robert and Hannah Harris, married Mary Ann Morrow, November, 1841. John was a "sadler" by trade, and we judge he must have been an expert in the business from a sample of his work he exhibited in the saddle he rode when in 1835 he visited Steele Creek, the home of his father's childhood.

John died at his home in Somerville, Ala., in 1880. His remains lie in the cemetery of that place. Eight children were born to John and Mary Ann Harris, Samuel Robert, Rosey Jane, Calvin Grier, Mary Etna, James Washington, Emily Jane, William Alexander and Margaret Ann. Samuel Robert, Rosy Jane and Emily Jane, all died very young.

Calvin Grier, third, but eldest living child of John and Mary Ann Harris married Lucy Bolling Campbell, in August, 1879. These parents have two children, Claude and Annie. Calvin Grier Harris, is the present Tax Assessor of Morgan County, Ala. He has held this office for the last sixteen years.

Mary Etna, fourth child of John and Mary Ann Harris, married Henry M. Mason, in November, 1877. Mary Etna died in 1879, leaving no children.

James Washington, fifth child of John and Mary Ann Harris, married Idella Emily Terry, in February, 1879. They have three children, Mary Sugars, Margaret Lapsley, and Terry Jackson. James Washington is the present commissioner of Revenue for Morgan County, Ala.

William Alexander, seventh child of John and Mary Ann Harris, married Minnie C. Pearce, in 1880. These parents have four children, Hardy Calvin, Edward, Eva and Johnie. The last named are both daughters.

Margaret Ann, eighth and youngest child of John and Mary Ann Harris, married William Pearce, in 1885. Death soon dissolved this union. William Pearce died in 1887, leaving no children.

Isabella, second child of Robert and Hannah Harris, married William D. Harper in August, 1836. Six children are the fruit of this union. John William, Amanda, Mallie, Martha Freeman, Samuel Harris and Jane.

John William, the eldest child of Isabella and William D. Harper, married Sarah Fowler, in 1866. They have four children, Eugene, Ernest, Jane and William.

Amanda, second child of Isabella and William D. Harper is unmarried.

Mallie Harper, third child of Isabella and William D. Harper, married Rufus Crenshaw in 1871. They have three children, Annie Bell, Gertrude and Claude.

Martha Freeman, fourth child of Isabella and William D. Harper, married Thomas F. Tusley in 1884. These parents have three children, names not given.

Samuel Harris Harper, fifth child of Isabella and William D. Harper, married Mamie Hinds in 1889. They have no children.

Jane Harper, sixth child of Isabella and William D. Harper, married Matthew Todd in 1884. They have one child, Matthew.

Martha, third child of Robert and Hannah Harris, married William A. Jones in 1842. Four children are the fruit of this union, John P., Mary, Hannah and William A. All are deceased except William A.

James Leroy, fourth child of Robert and Hannah Harris, married Emily Bush in 1848. The fruit of this union is five children, viz., Mary, John, James, William and Ida. After a thorough course of literary and theological training James Leroy entered the ministry of the Presbyterian Church. He is now located in Dallas, Texas.

Sarah Elizabeth, fifth child of Robert and Hannah Harris, was married to William Eperson, in 1848. Four children were born to these parents, viz., Martha Virginia, John Robert, Joseph D., and Charles C.

Martha Virginia, eldest child of Sarah Elizabeth and William Eperson, was married to John Coffey. We have no record of her family.

John Robert, second child of Sarah Elizabeth and William Eperson, entered Hampden Sidney College, Virginia, and after a full course graduated. He had decided to give himself to the ministry of the Presbyterian Church, but his hopes were not realized as an early death called him to a higher ministry in Heaven. He died the year of his graduation.

Joseph D., third child of Sarah Elizabeth and William Eperson, married Susan Jane Lynn in 1890. They have one child, Cora. Joseph D. Eperson is the present Treasurer of Morgan County, Ala., serving his second term.

Charles C., fourth child of Sarah Elizabeth and William Eperson, graduated from the South-Western

University, Clarksville, Tenn. He entered the ministry of the Presbyterian Church and is located at Lacan, Ala. His companion in life is Frances Morris. They have four children, viz., William W., Ernest, Elizabeth M., and Lula.

Amanda, sixth child of Robert and Hannah Harris, married Charles Jenkins in 1853. They have quite a family of children; names not given.

Cynthia Witherspoon, seventh child of Robert and Hannah Harris, was married to Dr. John Francis in 1852. The fruit of this union is nine children, Samuel Leroy, John William, Robert Orfield, James Leonard, George Edward, Matthew Witherspoon, Eleanor Idella, Mary Elva and Elizabeth.

Samuel Leroy, eldest son of Cynthia Witherspoon and Dr. Frances, married Mary Elizabeth Kilpatrick in 1876. They have two sons, Frances Otts and Edward Eugene.

William Robert, eighth and youngest child of Robert and Hannah Harris, entered the Confederate service and was killed at the battle of Seven Pines in Virginia in 1862, under the command of Stonewall Jackson.

Hugh Harris, fifth child of Hugh and Martha R. Harris, was born, November 22, 1791. He married Eleanor Harris, second child of John and Martha H. Harris, August 8, 1815. Eleanor was born October 14, 1792. Hugh settled near his father's home on the public road leading to Nation Ford on the Catawba River. He was at an early age elected and ordained ruling elder in Steele Creek Church, which office he filled with a conscientious devotion to duty. He was a Christian of the highest type, whose praise was in all the churches. His life came to a close on January 14, 1855, in the sixty-fourth year of his age. His remains lie in the Blackstock Cemetery. Hugh and Eleanor remained only a few years in their first home. The death of Eleanor's father, Captain John Harris, in September, 1824, necessitated a change, and they moved into the house with the widowed mother, that she might enjoy the loving ministration of her daughter in her declining years; but soon a change took place, for a malignant fever brought Eleanor's life to a close, October 30, 1828, in the thirty-sixth year of her age. She was buried in Big Steele Creek Cemetery. Eleanor was mother of the following children: John Leonard, born May 29, 1816; James Moore, born March 23, 1818; Hugh Clark, May 19, 1820; Rachel Clementina, and Martha Matilda.

John Leonard, oldest child of Hugh and Eleanor Harris, at an early age, accepted a clerkship in one of the old and reliable "firms" of Chester, and was connected with it for a number of years, and so became a permanent resident of Chester. Later he was elected cashier in the Bank of Chester, which position he held for more than thirty years. He was also prominent in all the work of the church, being a ruling elder in the Presbyterian church of Chester. John Leonard was married to Mary Ann Robertson, of Chester County, South Carolina, in May, 1850, and died on Monday, the 4th of July, 1892, in the seventy-sixth year of his age. Mary Ann Harris died in the Spring of 1856. The remains of both rest in the cemetery of Chester, South Carolina.

Two daughters were the fruit of this union, Mary and Eunice. Mary was born July, 1852. She married James Brawley, of Chester. To these parents were born eight children,—John Harris, who died in early manhood; Eunice, Annie, Mary, Rachel, Hiram, Henry and William Foote.

Eunice, youngest daughter of John Leonard and Mary Ann Harris, was born in 1855, married Norwood Obear, of the legal profession, of Winnsboro, S. C., a son of the late Rev. Obear, rector of the Episcopal church in Winnsboro. Their home was in Winnsboro for some years where Norwood Obear practiced his profession. He is now located in Washington, D. C. These parents have had four children, but only two survive, Joseph and Hugh Harris.

James Moore, second child of Hugh and Eleanor Harris, died August 29, 1829, in the eleventh year of his age.

Hugh Clark, third child of Hugh and Eleanor Harris, was married to Jane McCaule Harris, at the residence of her parents, in York County, S. C., December 22, 1841. She was a daughter of Col. James Harris, and grand daughter of Robert Harris, second son of John and Eleanor Reynolds Harris.

Hugh Clark Harris, owned by right of purchase, and occupied the "Home Place" of the "Historic

Pair," where they spent their last years, the dwelling being removed to a more elevated location in a beautiful grove. Hugh Clark was an efficient deacon in Steele Creek Church; was a man of many noble traits of character, of high social qualities, a good man in every sense of the word. His death took place in Steele Creek Church, an unusual place for such a scene, but a fitting place for a good man to be translated from the earthly to the heavenly sanctuary. He had been subject to some heart trouble, but was apparently in good health the day of his death. He, with others, assembled at church for Christian Conference, or what was formerly known in "Orthodox" churches as "Quarterly Examination." The pastor, Rev. James C. Chalmers, was conducting the exercises by question and answer, and just as the question, "What is faith in Jesus Christ?" was being discussed, with his eyes and attention fixed on his pastor, Hugh Clark's spirit departed. In a moment a physician, Dr. J. M. Strong, and others were at his side, only to realize that the vital spark had fled. He died April 2, 1879, in the fifty-ninth year of his age.

His wife, Jane M., had preceded him to the grave seventeen years. She was born May 2, 1814, and died November 4, 1862, aged forty-eight. Their bodies rest in the cemetery of Blackstock Church. These parents, Hugh C. and Jane M. Harris, had three daughters. Emma Rose, the eldest, died in the bloom of youth of typhoid fever, October 2, 1862, in the eighteenth year of her age. Her mother died one month later of the same disease. Mary Anna and Mason Ella are the surviving daughters.

Mary Anna, second daughter, was married at the residence of her father to James R. Miller, of York County, S. C., December 23, 1869, by Rev. James C. Chalmers. The fruit of this union is six children, all daughters, viz.: Kate Ross, Emma Jane, Addie Allison, Clark Harris, born May 1, 1879, died July 28, 1890; Robert Mason and Johnie.

Kate Ross, the eldest, married Charles Moore Strong, M. D. Their child is given under her husband's name.

Emma Jane graduated from the Due West Female College in 1892, and has a position in the graded school of Concord, N. C.

Mason Ella, youngest daughter of Hugh Clark and Jane M. Harris, was married at the residence of her father in York County, S. C., by Rev. James C. Chalmers, September 2, 1874, to Samuel J. Alexander, M. D., of Mecklinburg County, N. C., at that time a practicing physician in Steele Creek, and son of Isaac Alexander. He was educated at Davidson College, N. C., and graduated from the Charleston Medical College, South Carolina, in 1857. Dr. Alexander's married life was short, as he died at the residence of his father-in-law, Hugh C. Harris, of diphtheria, January 20, 1876. Mason Ella Alexander makes her home with her sister, Mary A. Miller, at the *old home*, once the home of the "Historic Pair."

These sisters, Mary Anna and Mason Ella, have a

double portion of "Harris" blood flowing in their veins. Three of their great-grandfathers were brothers, viz: Hugh, Robert and John, sons of John and Eleanor Reynolds Harris. Their paternal grand parents were Hugh and Eleanor Harris, Hugh being the son of Hugh Harris, Sr., and Eleanor, daughter of Captain John Harris. Their maternal grandfather was Colonel James Harris, son of Robert Harris.

Rachel Clementina, fourth child of Hugh and Eleanor Harris, was born, May 26, 1822, was married at her father's residence, by Rev. Isaac Grier, D. D., March 19, 1842, to William Boyce, a ruling elder in Steele Creek Church, and died on Sabbath, December 11, 1842, of pneumonia. Her remains rest in the cemetery at Blackstock Church.

Martha Matilda, the youngest child of Hugh and Eleanor Harris, was born December 21, 1824. Married John Orr of Mecklinburg County, N. C., and went West. She soon sickened and died, leaving one son, who died in boyhood. We have no dates.

Hugh Harris' second marriage was to Margaret Hemphill of Chester County, S. C., June 5, 1832. Margaret Hemphill Harris died January 23, 1847. Aged forty-five years. The fruit of this marriage was three children, Robert Hemphill, Eleanor Jeannette and Eliza Isabella.

Robert Hemphill, eldest child of Hugh and Margaret H. Harris, was born April 14, 1833. Robert H. inherited the "Home Place" of Captain John Harris and occupied for some years the same house, but later he erected a new dwelling a few hundred yards away in a grove, making a new settlement altogether, so none of the features of the old place can be recognized.

He was married, July 15, 1856, to Mary Eliza Query, daughter of Alexander Query of Steele Creek. She was born May 13, 1836. They have seven children: Hugh Whitfield, Elva Hemphill, born, December 12, 1859, died December 9, 1862; Robert Alexander, Margaret Elizabeth, Mary Isabella, Martha Jemima and Lois Jeannette.

Hugh Whitfield, eldest child of Robert H. and Mary Harris, was born July 7, 1857. He graduated from Erskine College, Due West, S. C., in July, 1878, with a major share of the honors of the class. Entered the legal profession, located at Charlotte, N. C., and is one of the rising lawyers of the city. He has also represented the County of Mecklinburg, N. C., in the Lower House of the Legislature. On the 24th of October, 1894, Hugh Whitfield Harris married Anna Gertrude Conrad of Forsythe County, N. C.

Robert Alexander, third child of Robert H. and Mary Harris, was born June 6, 1863; graduated at Erskine College, Due West, S. C., in 1883; located at West Point, Va., and is in the employ of the Southern Railway Co. He married Susan W. Courtney, of Virginia, June 27, 1893. The fruit of this union is one child, Mary, born October 24, 1894. Robert A. is a ruling elder in the General Assembly Presbyterian Church of West Point, Va.

Margaret Elizabeth, fourth child of Robert H. and Mary Harris, was born July 28, 1866, graduated from the Charlotte Female Institute in 1885, and was married by Rev. G. R. White at the residence of her parents in Steele Creek, York County, S. C., December 23, 1886, to Rev. Charles Edgar McDonald, then pastor of Steele Creek Associate Reformed Church. Charles Edgar is a son of the late Rev. L. McDonald, and was born near Richburg, Chester County, S. C., November 23, 1859. He connected with the Associate Reformed Church at Due West, S. C., during the period of his last year in College, May, 1877. He graduated from Erskine College July 4, 1877, and from the Theological Seminary at Due West, S. C., in June, 1881. He was licensed by the First Presbytery of the Synod of the South at Shiloh, Lancaster County, S. C., September 6, 1881, and ordained and installed pastor of Steele Creek Church, Mecklinburg County, N. C., November 3, 1882. Here he labored till April, 1892, when he demitted Steele Creek and accepted a call from Winnsboro Church, Fairfield County, S. C., the late charge of Rev. John T. Chalmers, who had removed to Philadelphia. He was installed by the First Presbytery in this charge, May 13, 1892. The only child of these parents, Rev. C. E. and Margaret Elizabeth McDonald, was Charles Stinson, who was born December 12, 1887, and died April 28, 1888, aged four months and sixteen days. Its remains lie in the cemetery of old Blackstock Church in York County, S. C.

It might be of interest to relate a somewhat unusual incident in connection with Rev. C. E. McDonald's respective pastorates. He was the immediate successor of the late Rev. James C. Chalmers, in his pastorate in Steele Creek, N. C., and in his pastorate of Winnsboro, S. C., he succeeded Rev. John T. Chalmers, son of Rev. James C. Chalmers.

Mary Isabella and Martha Jemima, daughters of Robert H. and Mary Eliza Harris, are graduates of the Charlotte Institute. Lois Jeannette, the youngest daughter, is a graduate of the Due West Female College of the class of 1892. All have been engaged in teaching at different periods since graduating.

Eleanor Jeannette, second child of Hugh and Margaret Hemphill, was born September 27, 1836. She was married to Morrison Caldwell, of Mecklinburg County, N. C., September 22, 1859, at the residence of her brother, Robert H. Harris, York County, S. C., by Rev. James C. Chalmers. The fruit of this union was one son, Morrison H., who was born August 23, 1860, and married Rosa McCorkle, of Salisbury, Rowan County, N. C., December 12, 1889.

Morrison Caldwell entered the Confederate service, was mortally wounded at the battle of Chancellorsville, Va., on May 3, 1862, and died on the 7th of May at the field hospital.

Eleanor Jeannette's second marriage was to Robert L. Query, of North Carolina, August 3, 1867. The fruit of this marriage is three children, Lena M., who was born April 26, 1868; Leonard, born November

11, 1871, and Mary Eliza, born June 30, 1875. They reside at Davidson College, N. C. Lena M. Query married Charles T. Dickinson of Bainbridge, Decatur County, Ga., son of George Dickinson, January 1, 1891. Their residence is in Bainbridge, Ga.

Eliza Isabella, third child of Hugh and Margaret Hemphill Harris, was born June 30, 1840. She was married at the residence of her brother, Robert H. Harris, in York County, S. C., by Rev. James C. Chalmers April 29, 1862, to J. Elam Caldwell, of Mecklinburg County, N. C. Eight children were born to these parents: Mary Elizabeth, July 25, 1863; Elva Hemphill, February 1, 1866; Eunice Jeannette, May 24, 1870; Robert William, March 25, 1873, and died March 2, 1874, aged one year; Margaret Louise, March 1, 1875; Eleanor Reynolds, May 8, 1877; Hugh Harris, March 5, 1880, and James Edwin, October 30, 1882.

Mary Elizabeth, eldest child of Isabella and J. Elam Caldwell, was married June 12, 1889, to Robert Franklin Grier, at Harrisburg, Mecklinburg County, N. C., a son of the late Major Zenas A. Grier, of Steele Creek, N. C. They have two children, Mary Isabella, born March 11, 1890, and Robert Franklin, Jr., born September 22, 1892. Elva Hemphill, second child of Isabella and J. Elam Caldwell, married William Edwin Harris, October 23, 1889, at the residence of her parents, at Harrisburg, N. C. Their only child, Ellen Hemphill, was born January 3, 1892. William Edwin Harris, is a descendent of another Harris family, of

Mecklinburg County, N. C., not connected with the Harris family under discussion. Hugh Harris' third marriage was to Mary Walker, of Mecklinburg County, N. C., January 28, 1851. Mary Walker Harris died May 24, 1874, in the seventy-fourth year of her age. Her remains lie beside those of her husband, in the Old Blackstock Cemetery.

CHAPTER VII.

JANE HARRIS PEOPLES, YOUNGEST CHILD OF HUGH HARRIS, SR., AND HER CHILDREN, HUGH HARRIS, JOHN BROWN, ISABELLA HUNTER, MATTEW HENRY, JAMES HARVEY AND RICHARD RAMSEY.

Jane, sixth child of Hugh Harris, Sr., and Martha R. Harris, was born in Mecklinburg County, N. C., May 18, 1798, and married at the residence of her parents in Mecklinburg County, N. C., in 1816 by Rev. Isaac Grier, D. D., to Richard Peoples, of the same county.

Richard Peoples was born July 26, 1790, and for many years held the office of ruling elder in Sardis church, N. C. He died November 23, 1870. Jane Peoples died December 14, 1872. Their remains lie in the cemetery at Sardis church, Mecklinburg County, N. C. They had ten children, Hugh Harris; John Brown; Isabella Hannah; Martha Eleanor, born October 23, 1823, died September 3, 1827; Leroy Ezekiel, born August 4, 1826, died November 2, 1858; Matthew Henry; Elizabeth Jane, born June 24, 1832, and died July 30, 1859; James Harvey; Isaac Newton, born February 15, 1837, who entered the Confederate service in 1862, returned home on a sick furlough, and died at his father's residence, September 6, 1862; and Richard Ramsey.

Hugh Harris, eldest child of Jane and Richard Peoples, was born March 29, 1817, and married Amanda Williamson, daughter of Cyrus Williamson, of Mecklinburg County. These parents had two children, William, who died in childhood, and Isabella Watson.

Isabella Watson was born August 9, 1859. She was married to Harris Green Lee Rea, of Providence, N. C., November 5, 1874. He was born June 7, 1853. These parents have ten children, viz., Carrie Watson, born November 11, 1875; Ada Elizabeth, September 14, 1877; Maybelle Lee, October 4, 1879; Emma Peoples, September 26, 1881; John Harris, October 25, 1883; Gertrude McDowel, July 25, 1885; Lester McLees, November 13, 1887; Edith Lorraine, September 15, 1889; Hugh Calvin, August 22, 1891; and Green Moffatt, born November 15, 1893.

John Brown, second child of Jane and Richard Peoples, was born, November 10, 1818. He was married to Mrs. Rebecca Montgomery Stitt (née Orr) of Mecklinburg County, N. C., August 25, 1846, who was born October 20, 1815, and died June 21, 1865.

John Brown was ordained a ruling elder at Laurel Springs, Ash County, N. C., in 1854, by Rev. John Hunter, who was then pastor. Upon his removing in 1859 to Ebenezer Associate Reformed Church, Tippah County, Mississippi, he was received as an elder and served the church in that capacity till death. During the war in visiting his step-son in the army, he contracted measles which resulted in his death, June 6,

1862. The cemetery at Ebenezer Church contains the remains of both husband and wife.

The fruit of this marriage was one child, Rachel Jane, who was born in Mecklinburg County, N. C., September 21, 1849. Rachel Jane was married in Sardis, Panola County, Mississippi, January 21, 1875, to Rev. S. A. Agnew, D. D., son of the late Enoch Agnew, M. D. Rev. Agnew was born in Abbeville County, S. C., November 22, 1833, graduated in Erskine College, Due West, S. C., August 11, 1852, under the Presidency of Rev. R. C. Grier, D. D. During the years 1854 and 1855 he was in attendance in the Erskine Theological Seminary at Due West, Rev. James P. Pressly being Chief Professor. He spent balance of time as a student of theology under the Superintendency of Rev. James L. Young; was licensed to preach the Gospel by the Associate Reformed Presbytery of Memphis at Troy, Tennessee, April 26, 1856; was ordained by the same Presbytery at Shiloh Church, Lafayette County, Miss., April 23, 1859; was installed pastor of Bethany Associate Reformed Church, Lee County, Miss., July 31, 1868, and Hopewell Associate Reformed Church, Union County, Miss., July 23, 1870. Rev. Samuel A. Agnew's relation to both of these churches has continued to the present time. The title of Doctor of Divinity was conferred by Erskine College.

Rachel Jane and Rev. Samuel A. Agnew, D. D., have nine children, viz: John Brown, born November 3, 1875; Mary Letitia Rebecca, born August 15, 1877, and died October 13, 1878; Margaret Elizabeth, born October 4, 1878, died April 6, 1861 ; Rutherford Todd, born October 14, 1880; Jane Ivanona, born September 21, 1882 ; Eleanor Simpson, born September 2, 1884; Samuel Andrew, born October 11, 1886; Isabella Montgomery, born May 19, 1890, and Richard Peoples, born March 24, 1893.

Isabella H. Peoples, third child of Richard and Jane Peoples, was born February 1, 1821, married Rev. John Hunter, of the Associate Reformed Church, July 18, 1843, a son of Thomas Hunter, of Mecklinburg County, N. C., and born November 13, 1814. John Hunter graduated from Jefferson College, Canonsburg, Pa., in the fall of 1841, under the Presidency of Dr. Matthew Brown. His theological course was for some time under the private instruction of Rev. J. G. Witherspoon, but completed in the Associate Reformed Seminary at Due West, S. C., in 1843. He was licensed at Union Church, S. C., April 19th of the same year; was ordained and installed over the congregation of Back Creek, Prosperity and Gilead, in Mecklinburg County, N. C., July 25, 1844. In 1854, he demitted this charge and spent four years in Ash County, N. C., on account of failing health, but doing missionary work as he was able. In 1858, he accepted a call from Sardis Church, Mecklinburg County, N. C., and was installed in the fall of that year. He demitted Sardis in the Spring of 1886, in consequence of a partial stroke of paralysis received in the pulpit at Thyatira, a branch of the Sardis Church.

Rev. John Hunter was married three times, first (as has been stated) to Isabella H. Peoples, who is the mother of all his children, and who died August 3, 1859, aged thirty-eight years. Her remains lie in the cemetery at Sardis. His second marriage was to Mrs. Martha Simonton Bell, of Fairfield County, S. C., December 10, 1861; born January 1, 1826, and died May 9, 1864, aged thirty-eight years. His third marriage was October 9, 1866, to Mary Ann McDill, of Chester County, S. C. She died June 27, 1894, aged sixty-nine years. Rev. John Hunter died May 16, 1890, in the seventy-sixth year of his age. His remains lie in Sardis Cemetery.

Isabella H. and Rev. John Hunter, were the parents of four children, Jane Eliza, Richard Brown, Margaret Alice, and Lester Walker.

Jane Eliza, the eldest child, was born September 14, 1846. She entered the Female College at Due West, S. C., with bright prospects of completing her education and of fitting herself for greater usefulness, but in a short time, however, symptoms of a pulmonary disease developed, and she was brought home to linger a few months and then fill an early grave. She died November 29, 1863.

Richard Brown, second child of Rev. John Hunter and Isabella, was born April 20, 1848. He took a partial course in Erskine College. He married Margaret Eleanor Cannon October 8, 1867, daughter of J. M. and Deborah Eliza Robison Cannon, a descendant of the same branch, (Hugh Harris, Sr.) They are both great-great grandchildren of the "Historic Couple." Richard Brown occupies his father's home place near to Sardis Church, Mecklinburg County, N. C.

Richard and Margaret E. Hunter have eight children, of whom six are living, Eliza Isabella, born December 10, 1868; Oscar Cannon, born November 20, 1870; Baxter Ross, born March 10; 1873; John Lester, born February 9, 1876; James Harris, born March 20, 1878; Daisie Eleanor, March 25, 1881, and died July 4, 1881, aged three months; Eunice Irene, born July 18, 1882, and Richard Brown, born February 3, 1887 and died June 17, 1887, age four months.

Eliza Isabella, first child of Richard and Margaret Hunter, married Ellis Alexander, June 8, 1887. They have two children, Lucy Cannon, born April 15, 1890, and Pauline, born September 16, 1891.

Baxter Ross, third child of Richard and Margaret Hunter, was educated at Erskine College, Due West, S. C., took a medical course at the Missouri Medical College, St. Louis, Mo.; and is located in Chester County, S. C., practicing his profession.

Margaret Alice, third child of Rev. John Hunter and Isabella was born September 13, 1850, married Simeon H. Huey, in the fall of 1869 and died December 6, 1875, aged twenty-five years.

Margaret Alice left two children, Frank Verner and Margaret.

Frank Verner married Lillian Gribble of Matthews, N. C., March, 1892; and they have one son, Charleton.

Lester Walker, fourth and youngest child of Rev. John Hunter and wife Isabella, was born July 26, 1853. After finishing the junior year in Erskine College, he began the study of medicine, graduating from Bellevue Hospital Medical College, New York City in March, 1875. He located in the vicinity in which he was reared, near to Sardis Church, Mecklinburg County, N. C., and is sucessfully practicing his profession. He is also a ruling elder in Sardis congregation. He married Martha Caroline, daughter of Dr. James Boyce and Martha H. Boyce, at the home of her parents in Due West on December 1, 1875. The ceremony was performed by Dr. Wm. L. Pressly, assisted by Dr. Wm. M. Grier. He and his brother Richard both married *great-great granddaughters* of the "Historic Couple," descendants of Hugh Harris, Sr. Martha Caroline was born October 1851. These parents have ten children, Mary Isabella, born October 6, 1879; Owen Livingston, born July 9, 1882; Helen Harris, born December 28, 1884; Louie and Louise, twins, born July 16, 1886; Alice, born December 8, 1887; James Boyce, born September 25, 1889; Lester Walker, born October 27, 1891, and died at eleven months old, and Moffatt and Merideth, twins, born June 16, 1893. Moffatt died aged six weeks, and Meridith died aged thirteen months.

Matthew Henry, sixth child of Jane and Richard Peoples, was born in Mecklinburg County, N. C., February 13, 1829. He was married October 14, 1852, to Margaret Adaline Neal, at the residence of her father,

General William Neal, in Steele Creek, Mecklinburg County, N. C. She was born March 1, 1832. Matthew Henry was a resident for a few years of Ash County, N. C. When the Mission Church of Laurel Springs of that county, conducted by Rev John Hunter, was dissolved, he removed to Iredell County, N. C., in the bounds of Rev. Wm. B. Pressly's charge. From that county he entered the Confederate service as a captain. He fell mortally wounded on June 27, 1862, and died July 2, 1862. His remains were brought home and interred in the cemetery at Sardis Church, N. C., in the bounds of which he was born and reared.

Very soon Margaret Adaline removed to Steele Creek, with her family of five small children, all too young to realize their loss, he youngest being only four months old. In Steele Creek her life came to a close, February 9, 1892. Her remains were interred in the cemetery at Big Steele Creek. Their children, six in number, are Emma Jane, born July, 30, 1853; William Neal, born June 9, 1855; infant daughter, born April 28, 1857, and died 1857; Richard Baxter, born May 27, 1858; Edgar Harris, born December, 24, 1860; Matthew Henry, born in Iredell County, N. C., February 22, 1862.

William Neal, second child of Matthew and M. Adaline Peoples, married Harriet Eugenia Smith, of Charlotte, N. C., December 5, 1878, the ceremony being performed by the late Rev. A. W. Miller, D. D., then pastor of the First Presbyterian Church, Charlotte, N. C.

Edgar Harris, son of Matthew H. and M. Adaline Peoples, was married to Lola May Strong, at the residence of her father, John M. Strong, M. D., in Steele Creek, N. C., by Rev. Charles E. McDonald, September, 1890. They have one child, Eleanor. Lola May is a descendant of Captain John Harris, third son of John and Eleanor.

Elizabeth Jane, seventh child of Jane and Richard Peoples, was born in Mecklinburg County, N. C., June 24, 1832, and died July 30, 1859. The two sisters, Elizabeth Jane, and Isabella H. Hunter, wife of Rev. John Hunter, died after a protracted illness. Isabella was taken to the house of her parents where she could have their constant and loving care, and be near an only sister, who was similarly afflicted. They peacefully passed away within three days of each other. "They were lovely and pleasant in their lives and in death they were not divided."

James Harvey, eighth child of Jane and Richard Peoples, was born in Mecklinburg County, N. C., November 22, 1834. He graduated from Erskine College in the Summer of 1856, Rev. R. C. Grier, D. D., President. Was licensed by the First Presbytery of the "Synod of the South" in April, 1860; ordained and installed pastor of Hopewell Congregation, Maury County, Tenn., by the Tennessee Presbytery, May, 1867; was released from this congregation in October, 1889, since which time he has supplied vacant churches.

His home is in Maury County, Tenn. Rev. James H. Peoples was married to Margaret Simonton Douglass, at the residence of her parents in Fairfield County, S. C., by Rev. James Boyce, D. D., April 24, 1862. She is a daughter of the late Alexander Douglass of Fairfield County, S. C.

The fruit of this marriage is nine children: Isaac Douglass, born January 28, 1863 and died July 6, 1864; Jane Simonton, born January 16, 1865; Minnie Harris, born January 17, 1867; Richard Grier, born in Maury County, Tenn., March 8, 1869; Robert Haldane, born in Maury County, Tenn., March 4, 1871; Margaret Jennette, born, November 3, 1874; James Alexander, February 5, 1877; Annie Elizabeth, November 29, 1878, and Edgar Livingston, November 17, 1881. Richard Grier graduated from Erskine College in June, 1884, and is Principal of an Institution at Bell Buckle, Maury County, Tenn. The two eldest daughters, Jennie Simonton and Minnie Harris, are graduates of the Due West Female College in the class of 1884. Isaac Newton, ninth child, was born February 15, 1837, and died September 6, 1862.

Richard Ramsey, tenth child of Jane and Richard Peoples, was born in Mecklinburg County, N. C., February 14, 1841. He occupied the "old home" on McAlpen's Creek, six miles south of Sardis Church, Is a ruling elder in Sardis Church, Rev. R. G. Miller. pastor. Richard Ramsey has been married three times, first by Rev. R. W. Brice to Agnes Ann McDill of Chester County, S. C., December 18, 1866, a daughter of the late Colonel James McDill of Chester County, S. C. She was born July 4, 1841, and died, October 15, 1867, leaving one child, Agnes Jane, born October 10, 1867. She was only five days old at her mother's death, was raised by her grandmother McDill, in Chester County, S. C., and was married at her residence on January 30, 1889, by Rev. John A. White to Rev. Thomas G. Boyce of the Associate Reformed Church, son of the late Samuel Boyce of Sardis Church, Mecklinburg County, N. C.

Thomas Boyce was born February 3, 1862; graduated from Erskine College, South Carolina, June, 1885; entered the Theological Seminary at Due West in October of the same year; was licensed by the First Presbytery of the "Synod of the South," April 4, 1887, and graduated from the Seminary, May, 1888. Accepting calls from Hickory Spring and Shady Grove Churches, in the State of Arkansas, he was ordained and installed pastor of these churches by the Arkansas Presbytery, December 4, 1888. The relation was dissolved in 1893, and he was transferred to the Memphis Presbytery, and by it, installed pastor of Salem Associate Reformed Church, Tipton County, Tenn., March 3, 1893.

Agnes Jane and Rev. T. G. Boyce, have two children, James Harvey, born November 1, 1889; and Iva Theresa, born November 26, 1891.

Richard Ramsey Peoples' second marriage was to Margaret Elizabeth Montgomery, January 20, 1869, daughter of James Montgomery. She was born June

3, 1840, and died March 8, 1885. Their children are Mary Elizabeth, born December 9, 1869, died October 14, 1872; James McDill, born January 14, 1873; John Brown, born June 20, 1876; and Isabella Montgomery, born August 15, 1878.

Richard Ramsey's third marriage was to Margaret Amanda Wylie, February 9, 1886, daughter of the late John Wylie, of York County, S. C. Margaret Amanda was born in 1839.

This closes, so far as our information goes, the record of the descendants of Hugh Harris, eldest son of John and Eleanor Reynolds Harris. Some were partial to their "kith and kin," several of the families overlapping by intermarriage. We find one in the legal profession, six who have chosen medicine as their field of usefulness, and quite a number in the ministry. The following lineal descendants entered this profession: R. C. Grier, W. M. Grier, B. H. Grier, M. B. Grier, R. Livy Grier, R. Leroy Grier, J. S. Grier, J. J. Grier, J. H. Peoples, H. H. Robison, J. F. Cannon, J. L. Harris and C. E. Eperson. Livingston Grier and J. R. Eperson died in course of preparation for the ministry, fifteen in all.

The following preachers are connected by marriage: Isaac Grier, J. G. Witherspoon, James Boyce, John Hunter, S. A. Agnew, T. G. Boyce, J. E. Martin, G. R. White, D. B. Pressly, J. S. Moffatt, C. E. McDonald, R. W. Mills, A. E. Sample and D. W. Wiseman, fourteen, making a total of twenty-nine.

It is indeed gratifying that so many can be classed

under the impressive and beautiful imagery of the Prophet, and repeated by the great Apostle: "How beautiful are the feet of them that preach the gospel of peace, and bring glad tidings of good things."

CHAPTER VIII.

DESCENDANTS OF ROBERT HARRIS, SECOND SON OF JOHN AND ELEANOR REYNOLDS HARRIS.

Robert, second son of John and Eleanor Harris, was born in Lancaster County, Pa., in 1756. He, with his brother Hugh, was in service during the Revolutionary War. Robert purchased a part of that extensive body of land owned by the Polks of North Carolina, that lay partly in Mecklinburg County, N. C., and York District, S. C., and was known as the "Polk land," his purchase being from that section that lay in York District, S. C., six or seven miles south of where his father and brothers located and immediately on the Catawba River. His dwelling was in full view of the river. Here he lived and died. He was married to Jane McCaule in 1779, who was born in 1758, a daughter of Rev. Thomas Harris McCaule.

During the Revolutionary War the Rev. Thomas Harris McCaule, was pastor of that large Presbyterian congregation, "Centre," in Mecklinburg County, N. C. He was a graduate of Princeton College, New Jersey, and was ordained in 1776. "Scarce of medium height, a stout frame and full body, with dark piercing eyes, a pleasant countenance and winning manners, with a fine voice; he was popular both as a preacher and as a man.

Public spirited, he encouraged the Revolution

* * * * went with his flock to the camp and was at the side of General Wm. Davidson when he fell at Cowan's Ford on the Catawba River, gallantly resisting Cornwallis. His classical attainments were such, that after the peace, when Mount Zion College was established in Winnsborough, S. C. he was made its principal professor," (*Foote's History of Presbyterianism in North Carolina.*) He was also trustee of "Liberty Hall Academy," located in Charlotte, N. C., chartered by the Legislature of North Carolina after the Revolutionary War began. "Foote" also says; "The preeminence of 'Liberty Hall,' as supplying the place of a college for the South, was transfered to Mount Zion College, Winnsborough, S. C., over which the Rev. Thomas Harris McCaule, the pastor of Centre congregation for some years and trustee of Liberty Hall, presided." During his presidency of the college, sons of prominent men from all parts of South Carolina, attended the college. He retired from the college in July 20, 1793, and died in connection with the South Carolina Presbytery in 1796.

A venerable lady of Charleston, S. C., whose father graduated in Mount Zion College under the presidency of Rev. T. Harris McCaule, says: "My father often spoke of him in terms of warmest commendation, regarding him as a man eminently fitted for the position he held, being highly educated and remarkably pious."

Robert Harris connected with the Presbyterian Church, and was present at the organization of Unity

Church, a few miles distant from his home, now called Fort Mill, York County, S. C. He was elected and ordained one of the ruling elders at its organization about 1788. This position he filled until his death, which occured September 28, 1841, in the eighty-fifth year of his age, a period of fifty-three years. His wife, Jane McCaule Harris died January 24, 1816, aged fifty-eight years. The remains of both lie in the cemetery at Fort Mill Church. We regret our inability to give the order of birth of Robert Harris' children, having secured the date of a part only of the family. Faithful efforts were made to procure the reliable record of the "Old Family Bible," but failed to do so, hence, cannot give dates and order.

Robert and Jane McCaule Harris were the parents of nine children, namely, Eleanor, James, Josiah, Malinda, Nancy, Robert, Hugh, John and Brown Lee.

Eleanor, eldest child of Robert and Jane McCaule Harris, was born April 7, 1781. She was married at the residence of her parents, August 14, 1806, to James McKee, who was born October 5, 1783. In later years he was elected and ordained a ruling elder in Unity Presbyterian Church, now Fort Mill. He died January 18, 1851, aged sixty-eight years.

Eleanor McKee died May 12, 1850, aged sixty-nine years. Their remains lie in the cemetery at Fort Mill, S. C. Eleanor and James McKee are the parents of ten children only four of whom lived to rear families; Samuel, born in 1807; Robert Harris, born December 25, 1808, died April 1, 1827; William, born December

14, 1810, killed July 17, 1838; Edwin Leroy, born October 7, 1812, died August 4, 1839; Eleanor Louisa Clark, and James Morrison, *twins*, born September 21, 1814; Josiah Alexander, born July 21, 1816, died November 27, 1838; Isaac Chauncy, born August 4, 1818, died April 5, 1820; Margaret Jane, born April 15, 1820; and John Brown, born February 23, 1823, died June 28, 1839.

Samuel, eldest child of Eleanor and James McKee, was married to Cynthia C. Morrison, May 7, 1835. She was sister to Rev. James Morrison of Virginia, and was in a lineal way connected with "Mary Moore" of Revolutionary fame.

These parents, Samuel and Cynthia McKee, have two children, Mary Eleanor and Louisa. Mary Eleanor married Wm. Leeve. Samuel resided in Lowndes County, Ala., and died there June 10, 1842, in the thirty-fifth year of his age. Cynthia McKee after the death of her husband removed to Pensacola Florida.

James Morrison, fifth child of Eleanor and James McKee, was born in York County, S. C., September 21, 1814, a twin with Louisa. In his youth he accompanied his older brother, Samuel, to Alabama. There he entered the ministry of the Presbyterian Church. His labors were principally confined to that state.

His daughter writes: "My father was a member of South and East Alabama Presbytery for thirty years and more. When he died he was one of East Alabama's most honored and loved members. He graduated at no college, having received most of his literary and common school education, as well as languages at Ebenezer Academy, near Yorkville, S. C. Neither do I think he was in a Theological Seminary. If at all, it was only for a short time. He studied with Rev. Wm. Martin at Sandy Ridge, Lowndes County, Ala. He was a fine Greek, Latin and Hebrew scholar and was always a hard student." He preached for a short time in Charlotte, N. C., but his only pastorates were in the state of Alabama. He was for a period of ten years pastor of the large country church at Sandy Ridge, Lowndes County. He was pastor also of Orian and Providence churches for ten or fifteen years. His daughter again says: "His last work was in the evangelistic field in the East Alabama Presbytery. In this his whole heart was engaged, travelling in the least settled districts, without thought of fatigue or personal comfort, his deep-toned piety and well-rounded Christianity were well known.". During his labors in this field his work came suddenly to a close, for entering a swollen stream he was drowned May 4, 1869.

Rev. James Morrison McKee was twice married; first to Susan F. Cook, of Haynesville, Lowndes County, Ala. The fruit of this union was two sons, James Payson and Edward Hampton, both of whom lost their lives in the late war. James was killed in Virginia at Port Republic. Edward Hampton, who was an unusually fine mathematician and had studied civil engineering before the war, died in the hospital of Camp Measles. Neither of these brothers was married.

Rev. James M. McKee's second marriage was to Mrs. Olivia H. Olmstead, of Floyd, New York, December 4, 1842, at Selma, Ala. The fruit of this union was five children, three of whom are living, Edwin Leroy, Harvey Lloyd and Caroline Louisa. John McPherson, born March 5, 1851, died January 4, 1880; and William Henry, born June 18, 1855, died in infancy.

Edwin Leroy, eldest child of Rev. Jas. McKee, was born in Alabama, November 3, 1843, and was married December 26, 1878, to M. C. Courtney of Louisiana, daughter of J. S. Courtney. She was born September 24, 1850. These parents have three children: Eddie Courtney, born December 10, 1879; William Leroy, born June 21, 1882, and Ethel Louisiana, born April 29, 1884. Edwin Leroy has been a farmer, but is now in business in Cahaba, Ala.

Harvey Lloyd, second child of Rev. James and Olivia McKee was born in Alabama March 9, 1845. He was married May 13, 1869, to Mary Emma Evans, of Alabama. Harvey is a ruling elder in the Alabama Street Presbyterian Church, Selma, Ala. Five children were born to these parents, viz., Augusta S., February 1, 1869; James M., October 4, 1872; John M., February 9, 1876; Harvey L., May 26, 1879, and Howard R., born December 5, 1883, and died March 9, 1885.

Caroline Louisa, third child of Rev. James M. and Olivia McKee, was born in Alabama December 13, 1848, and was married May 5, 1868, to Charles Ward Hooper of Georgia, who was born May 24, 1843. He is a ruling elder in the First or Broad Street Presbyterian Church, Selma, Ala. The fruit of this union is ten children: Lloyd McKee born April 13, 1869; William, September 17, 1872, and died May 22, 1874; Olive, January 6, 1874; Caroline Edith, August 26, 1876; Ada Byrd, January 20, 1879; May, March 9, 1881; Charles Morrison, October 1, 1883, and died October 24, 1885; Harvey Lowry, July 28, 1885; James Jefferson, February 25, 1890, and Elsey Kay, August 4, 1892.

Lloyd McKee Hooper, the eldest of these children was married October 19, 1894, to Anna Steel Coleman of Alabama. Their home is in Selma, Ala.

Eleanor Louisa Clark, daughter of Eleanor and James McKee, a twin with James Morrison, was married to Robert H. Fullwood, of York County, S. C., May 12, 1836. Robert H. Fullwood was born March 9, 1801, and died July 29, 1871. Eleanor Louisa died July 24, 1845. These parents had six children, only two of whom lived beyond infancy, Robert H., born December 24, 1836, and Frances Ellen, October 30, 1839, and died October 12, 1843.

Robert H., the eldest child of Eleanor Louisa and Robert H. Fullwood, married December, 1859, Frances Elizabeth Harris, daughter of Stanhope A. Harris, a grandson of Robert Harris, Sr. The children of these parents are eight in number, William, Lee, Edward, Samuel, Hope, Gad, Lilla and Frank.

Edward, third child of Robert H. and F. E. Fullwood married Jennie ———, and they have one child, Robert.

Lilla, youngest daughter of Robert H. and Frances Elizabeth Fullwood, married Morrison Faris. They have two children, Viola and Guy. Robert H. Fullwood removed to Texas, and the entire family are residents of that state.

Margaret Jane, ninth child of Eleanor and James McKee, was married at the residence of her parents in York County, S. C., November 14, 1844, to Thomas Dryden Spratt, a graduate of South Carolina College, class of 1825, of the same county, who was born November, 8, 1804, and died April 3, 1884. Margaret Jane died December 17, 1887. Their remains lie in the cemetery at Fort Mill, S. C. Eight children were born to these parents, James, August 12, 1845; Thomas, July 14, 1847; John McKee, April 23, 1849; Barnett McRea, May 3, 1851; Eleanor, born February 27, 1853, and died September 16, 1854; Mary Anna, September 16, 1855; Margaret Ida, July 10, 1857; and Walter Edwin, January, 10, 1860.

James, eldest son of Margaret Jane and Thomas D. Spratt, entered Davidson College, North Carolina, in 1868, graduating in 1871. In the autumn of 1871 he entered the Theological Seminary in Columbia, S. C., and after a three years course graduated in 1874, and was licensed during that year by the Bethel Presbytery and was ordained by the same Presbytery in 1875.

For some years he was pastor of Hopewell Church in York County, S. C. He also supplied Six Mile Creek Church, in Lancaster County, giving half his time to each church. After his resignation of these churches, he devoted his time to the instruction of the colored people, both preaching to them and teaching.

He removed from his native state in 1888, and is now located in Collingsworth, Ky. On account of a conscientious change of views on some points of Christian faith and practice, he changed his ecclesiastical relations and is now preaching in connection with the Baptist Church in Collingsworth, and is also teaching.

James was married to Rosanna Cairns, in 1883. One son, Zacheus, is the fruit of this union, who was born November, 1884. Rosanna C. Spratt, died December 17, 1887. When the shadow of death fell across his threshold, it brought a double bereavement. It shut out the light of two homes. During Rosanna's last sickness his own dear mother left her home and came to minister to her comfort. In a short time she was stricken with pneumonia, and after a few days of suffering passed away the same day that Rosanna departed, and almost at the same hour, so they were not long separated.

It is a day long to be remembered by friends, and the congregation of Fort Mill, when two caskets with their precious contents were brought into the church and placed side by side, and after the solemn exercises conducted by the pastor, Rev. J. H. Thornwell, were borne away to the cemetery, there again to rest side by side until the morning of the Resurrection.

John McKee, third child of Margaret Jane, and

Thomas Dryden Spratt, was born April 23, 1849. He is President and Treasurer of the "Spratt Machine Company," located at Fort Mill, S. C., and has been one of the ruling elders in the Fort Mill Presbyterian Church for a number of years, Rev. J. H. Thornwell pastor. He was married to Susan Elizabeth Massey November 2, 1876. They have two children, Thomas Benjamin born April 22, 1878, who is now pursuing his education in the Citadel Academy, in Charleston, S. C., and John Leonidas, born April 3, 1880.

Barnett McRea, fourth child of Margaret Jane and Thomas D. Spratt, was born May 3, 1851. He makes his home in Chester, S. C., and has been connected for many years with the Chester Bank. In October, 1875, he was married to Frances Killian of Chester, S. C. They have nine children, Royden, born November 19, 1876; Julia, February 12, 1878; Barnett McRea, Jr., February 9, 1880; Frank, March 23, 1882; Kittie, March 7, 1884; John, March 5, 1886; Campbell, October 4, 1888; Fannie, March 5, 1891; and Thomas, born November 28, 1893.

Eleanor, fifth child of Margaret Jane and Thomas D. Spratt, was born February 27, 1853 and, died September 16, 1854.

Mary Ann, sixth child of M. Jane and Thomas D. Spratt was born September 16, 1855, and married William B. Hoke, January, 1880. Five children are the fruit of this union, John Spratt, born November 7, 1880; Margaret Ida, January 21, 1882, and died February 8, 1888; Joseph McKee, February 13, 1884;

Willie May, August 11, 1886, and Paul White, October 22, 1889.

Walter Edwin, eighth and youngest child of M. Jane and Thomas D. Spratt, was born January 10, 1860. His home is in Fort Mill, S. C., and he is connected with the "Spratt Machine Company." He married Martha Jane Belk, March, 1885. They have five children, James Dryden, born December, 11, 1885, and died June 30, 1886; Robbie Barnetta, September 7, 1887; John Thornwell, October 18, 1889; Infant daughter, November 8, and died November 8, 1890, and Elizabeth Ida, September 12, 1893. Walter Edwin is a deacon in the Fort Mill Presbyterian Church.

James M., son of Robert and Jane McCaule Harris, was born September 18, 1783. He was married to Frances Farrar in 1808, who was born September 26, 1786, and died November 14, 1850, aged sixty-four. James M. Harris died February 18, 1857, aged seventy-four. James Harris was at one time a ruling elder in Unity Church. Their remains lie in the cemetery at Fort Mill, S. C.

The fruit of this union was ten children, viz: Franklin H., Sarah F., Alfred Leroy, Jane McCaule, James Wallace, Stanhope A., Mary L., Robert P., Margaret E., and Rebecca Addie.

Franklin H., the eldest child of James and Frances Harris, was born October 29, 1809, married Martha Carothers, and died August 29, 1862, in his forty-seventh year. They had four children, James W., Margaret, Frances and Elisha.

James W., the eldest, was married to Margaret Ella Blankenship, at the residence of her mother in Mecklinburg County, N. C., October 19, 1871, by Rev. James C. Chalmers. Margaret Ella was a great-great-granddaughter of Captain John Harris. She died in 1874, leaving only one child, Frances Gertrude, born August 31, 1872. Frances Gertrude married Milas Milton Harkey, of Pineville, N. C., Semptember 20, 1893, the ceremony being performed by Rev. J. T. Wade. They have one child, Zebulon Vance, born September 12, 1894.

James W. Harris' second marriage was to Mrs. Potts, of York County, S. C., in 1876. The following are the children of this marriage: James Franklin, born September 21, 1878; Clyde Neely,———8, 1881; Charlton Bowen, June 27, 1884; Clarence C., June 7, 1887; and Mary Jane, August 28, 1890.

Margaret, second child of Franklin and Martha Harris, married J. M. Blankenship, D.D. S. She died early after her marriage, leaving one child, Minnie Hester, who married Robert Harris, a descendant of Captain John Harris. Her children are given under their father's name. J. M. Blankenship's second marriage was to Miss Yarborough.

Frances, third child of Franklin and Martha Harris, married John Kell. Their children are Elisha and Frank.

Elisha, youngest child of Franklin and Martha Harris, married Eliza Grant.

Sarah F., second child of James and Frances Harris,

was born October 24, 1810. She married Alfred Hutchison. Sarah F. died November 29, 1861. Her children are Malinda, Mary, Jane and James.

Mary, second child of Sarah F. and Alfred Hutchison, married Westly Wimble.

Jane married Joseph McCorkle.

Alfred Leroy, third child of James and Frances Harris, was born October 10, 1812, and died March 9, 1830, in the eighteenth year of his age.

Jane McCaule, fourth child of James and Frances Harris, married Hugh Clark Harris, a grandson of Captain John Harris. Her children will be given under her husband's name.

James Wallace, fifth child of James and Frances Harris, was born May 2, 1814, married Miss Bromfield, and was killed July 20, 1838.

Stanhope Alexander, sixth child of James and Frances Harris, was born August 9, 1818, and died May 10, 1890. Stanhope was twice married, first to Martha Rebecca McCullough, December 22, 1840, who was born December 30, 1821, and died April 13, 1860. Their children are Frances Elizabeth, born June 11, 1841; Martha Jane, December 24, 1843; Ella Eugenia, April 2, 1846, and died August, 1853; John Robert, April 24, 1848; Mary Anna, January 22, 1852, and died October 9, 1853; Cynthia Medora, November 28, 1855; and Sarah Adaline, March 8, 1858.

Frances Elizabeth, the first child of Stanhope Alexander and M. Rebecca Harris, married Robert H.

Fullwood of the same branch with herself, viz., Robert Harris, Sr. Her children are given under their father's name.

Martha Jane, second child of Stanhope Alexander and M. Rebecca Harris, married John Thompson, and died December 15, 1873.

John Robert, fourth child of Stanhope A. and M. Rebecca Harris, married Alice Irene Fullwood, December 16, 1869. John Robert died April 11, 1888. Alice Irene was the daughter of Robert H. Fullwood, Sr., by his first marriage. John Robert and Alice Irene Harris have eight children: Azile, born March 29, 1871, and married J. C. Hughs December 16, 1892; Daisy, June 19, 1872; Louisa, February 12, 1874; Robert, March 22, 1876; Mason, April 1, 1879; Laura, December 10, 1880, and died May 25, 1888; John, November 24, 1884, and Frances, July 24, 1886.

Cynthia Medora, eighth child of Stanhope A. and M. Rebecca Harris, married Lewis Bradford. Cynthia M. died February 5, 1874, leaving one child, Guy, also deceased.

Stanhope Alexander Harris' second marriage was to Mary Ann Fullwood April 4, 1862, daughter of Robert H. Fullwood, Sr. One child is the fruit of this marriage, Dovie Cornelia, born January 10, 1862.

Mary L., seventh child of James and Frances Harris, was born June 18, 1820, and died December 22, 1859. She was married to William Simril of York County, S. C. Their children are Sarah, Delia, Napoleon, James, Ida, Virginia and John.

Sarah, the eldest child of Mary L. and Wm. Simril, married David Barron.

Delia, second child of Mary L. and Wm. Simril, married Jefferson Lumpkin. Their children are Lottie and Laddie.

Napoleon, third child of Mary L. and Wm. Simril, married Mary Matthews.

Ida, fifth child of Mary L. and Wm. Simril, married James Matthews.

Virginia, sixth child of Mary L. and Wm. Simril, married Robert Glenn.

Robert P., eighth child of James and Frances Harris, was born January 17, 1823, and died in early manhood.

Margaret Eleanor, ninth child of James and Frances Harris, was born March 20, 1825, and died March 3, 1852, in the twenty-seventh year of her age. She married Franklin Carothers, of York County, S. C., a ruling elder in the Ebenezer Presbyterian Church. Their children are Stanhope, who died early in life, and Samuel A., who married Mary Erwin, daughter of the late Randolph Erwin, of Renalsburg, Mecklinburg County, N. C. Samuel A. Carothers was born September 28, 1848, and was married to Mary Erwin, November 14, 1872. He was a ruling elder in Pleasant Hill Presbyterian Church, Mecklinburg County, N. C., and died March 20, 1890. His remains lie in the cemetery of Pleasant Hill. Eight children were born to these parents: Randolph Erwin, November 21, 1874, Thomas Frank, April 2, 1876; Eddie, January 28,

1878, and died in childhood; Mary Harris, January 27, 1880; John McLean, August 29, 1881; Clarence Clyde, January 28, 1883; Harald Robinson, February 3, 1886, and Clara Adaline, September 24, 1887.

Rebecca Addie, tenth child of James and Frances Harris, was born January 31, 1831, and died August 6, 1874. She was married to Oliver R. Perry, M. D., August 7, 1851. He was born April 23, 1823, graduated from the Medical College in Charleston, S. C., in 1850, and located in Lancaster County, S. C. Dr. Perry died in 1858, and Rebecca Addie was left with four children, all too young to realize their loss. The eldest, Irene, was born August 23, 1852; Jack, August 18, 1855; Minnie Estelle, June 25, 1857, and Oliver R., August 29, 1859.

Malinda, second daughter of Robert and Jane McCaule Harris, married Aquilla Dyson. For some years they were residents of York County, S. C., and had quite a large family of children. They moved west and were lost sight of by the kindred. Jane, their eldest daughter, married Mr. Clark, of Tennessee, and died early after her marriage.

Nancy, third daughter of Robert and Jane McCaule Harris, married Mr. Thompson. Some children were born to these parents, but they removed west, and nothing definite is known of the family.

Josiah, son of Robert and Jane McCaule Harris, entered the ministry of the Presbyterian Church. He was taken under the care of Bethel Presbytery of the "Synod of South Carolina." After a course of theological training he was, by the Bethel Presbytery, licensed and ordained. Accepting a call from Unity Church, the church in which he was baptized and reared and in which his venerable father was a ruling elder, he was installed as pastor by the same Presbytery. After serving this church for sometime, he retired from the ministry and devoted himself to teaching. He married Elizabeth Sadler, of York County, S. C. They removed to Alabama, where they died, leaving no children.

Robert, son of Robert and Jane McCaule Harris, married Matilda Sadler, of York County, S. C. Robert died early in his married life, leaving no children. Matilda married, after some years, Mr. Harris, of Concord, N. C. Some of her descendants are now residents of Charlotte, N. C.

John, son of Robert and Jane McCaule Harris, died, having never married.

Hugh Harris, son of Robert and Jane McCaule Harris, was born in York County, S. C., March 12, 1800, and died August 27, 1839. Hugh was twice married, first to Elizabeth T. Stitt, of Providence, Mecklinburg County, N. C., March 3, 1825. She was born May 7, 1803. The fruit of this union was four children, Amelia Jane, born January 19, 1826, and died October 8, 1828, aged two years and ten months; Margaret Malinda; James Taylor, born February 26, 1830, and died December 27, 1833, aged three years and ten months; and John Stitt.

Elizabeth Stitt Harris, the mother of these children, died December 15, 1833, in the thirty-first year of her age.

Margaret Malinda, second child of Hugh and Elizabeth S. Harris, was born February 13, 1828, and married Joseph Doby of York County, S. C. They removed to the state of Arkansas, where Margaret M. died in 1861. Their children are Elizabeth Crawford and Margaret Harris.

Elizabeth Crawford married Charles K. Boswell. Their children are Joseph Kingston, Mary Elizabeth, and Grace.

Margaret Harris, youngest daughter of Margaret M. and Joseph Doby, married May 31, 1881, Rev. G. W. Davies, of the General Assembly Presbyterian Church, South. He graduated from Hampden Sydney College, Virginia, in 1875, Rev. J. M. P. Atkinson, President. He entered Union Theological Seminary, Virginia, graduating in 1880. He was licensed the same year. Accepting a call from Carolina Church, Arkansas, he was ordained and installed pastor by the Presbytery of Ouchita in 1881. These parents have three children, viz., Josie O., Banks and Jessie.

John Stitt, youngest child of Hugh and Elizabeth Stitt Harris, was born in the bounds of Providence Church, Mecklinburg County, N. C., August 1, 1832. At the death of his mother, John Stitt was a little over a year old and he was taken home and reared by his maternal uncle, Colonel John Stitt, whose wife was sister of Rev. Samuel Williamson, D.D., then pastor of Providence Church, and later, President of Davidson College,

N. C. He began his preparation for college at fourteen years of age. In 1849 he entered the Sophomore class in Davidson College, North Carolina, graduating in 1852, with the highest honor of his class. During his college life he made a public profession of religion and connected with Providence Church. In 1853 he entered the Theological Seminary at Columbia, S. C., and was connected with the Seminary for four years under Dr. J. H. Thornwell. In the third year of his course in the Seminary, 1856, he was licensed by the Concord Presbytery, of the North Carolina Synod. During the fourth year in the Seminary he supplied, by invitation, Bethesda Church, York County, S. C., and at the close of his theological course accepted a call from Bethesda congregation, was transferred from Concord Presbytery, North Carolina, to Bethel Presbytery, South Carolina, and by the latter ordained and installed pastor of Bethesda, April 16, 1857. He was the beloved and devoted pastor of this church for the period of seven years. For eighteen months he was laid aside from the active duties of the ministry by that "insidious and flattering disease, consumption." His spirit passed gently away on the evening of November 16, 1864, in the thirty-second year of his age. His remains lie in the cemetery at Bethesda Church.

Rev. John Stitt Harris, was married to Agnes Bratton, April 22, 1857, at the residence of her father, John S. Bratton, M. D., at Brattonville, York County, S. C. Five children were the fruit of this happy union. An only son, Myron, preceded his father to the grave. Four daughters survive. The eldest, Annie Elizabeth. married John E. Lowry, of Yorkville, S. C. Four children were born to these parents, James, Lucile Elizabeth, Adelia Annice, and John Harris, who died May 11, 1893.

Corinna, second daughter of Rev. J. S. and Agnes Harris, married Allen E. Gray, of Charlotte, N. C. Their children are four in number, Connie, John Harris, Eugene and Grace.

Margaret, third daughter of Rev. J. S. and Agnes Harris, married Oscar E. Thomas, druggist, of Columbia, S. C. They have four children, Ernest, Margaret, who died in 1893, Haleot and Agnes.

Agnes Stitt, fourth daughter of Rev. J. S. and Agnes Harris, married Frank Eugene Sims of Columbia, S. C. They have one child, Frank Eugene Sims, Jr. Agnes Bratton Harris, and her three youngest daughters and their families reside in Columbia, S. C. The eldest daughter has her home in Danville, Va.

Hugh Harris' second marriage was to Jane H. Matthews of Providence, Mecklinburg County, N. C., September 10, 1835, who was born August 2, 1818. The fruit of this second marriage was two children, Elizabeth Jane and Eleanor Ann.

Elizabeth Jane was born in Providence, July 12, 1836. She was married May 13, 1851, to Rev. James McCullough Walker, of the Associate Reformed Church, son of Hon. John Walker of Mecklinburg County, N. C., and born November 1, 1829. His father was for many years a ruling elder in Sardis Church. After his academical studies were completed, James McCullough Walker entered Davidson College, North Carolina, graduating with honor in 1847. He soon entered the Theological Seminary of the Associate Reformed Church at Due West, S. C., graduating in 1849. In September of the same year he was licensed by the First Presbytery of the "Associate Reformed Synod of the South." By order of the Synod he spent some months in supplying the mission of the "Synod of the South" in Nashville, Tenn. Accepting a call from Sardis Church, North Carolina, he was ordained and installed by the First Presbytery, May 9, 1851. Here he labored until 1858 when he changed his ecclesiastical relations and connected with the Concord Presbytery of the General Assembly Presbyterian Church. For sometime he supplied the Lancaster and Waxhaw churches. In 1859 he took charge of Philadelphia Church, North Carolina. His labors here were for a short period. He died at his residence in Mecklinburg County, N. C., of typhoid fever April 15, 1860. His remains lie in the cemetery at Sardis Church, in the bounds of which he was born and reared and where he first proclaimed the Gospel as pastor.

The funeral sermon of Rev. Walker was preached from 2 Sam. I : 26, by Rev. J. B. Watt, who had recently gone from the Associate Reformed Church to the Presbyterian Church and who died with typhoid fever a few months later, August, 1860.

The children of Elizabeth Jane and Rev. James M. Walker are Edgar Harris, Susan Laura, born March

26, 1854, and died November 27, 1854, aged eight months; John Washington, born May 16, 1856, and died April 17, 1860, following his father to the grave in two days; and Mary Jane Estelle.

Edgar Harris, eldest child of Elizabeth J. and Rev. J. M. Walker, was born April 27, 1852, graduated from Erskine College, South Carolina, and was married by Rev. Murray, of Greenwood, S. C., December 26, 1871, to Elizabeth R. Lomax, of Abbeville County, S. C., who was born August 10, 1855.

The children of these parents are Susan Bertha, born October 28, 1872; James Erling, August 16, 1874, who, in a competitive examination for Annapolis Naval Academy, received the appointment, standing highest above a number of applicants; John McCullough, September 4, 1876; and William Lomax, January 20, 1878.

Edgar Harris Walker is a resident of Charlotte, N. C., holding the office of County Treasurer.

Mary Jane Estelle, youngest child of Elizabeth and Rev. James M. Walker, was born July 31, 1858. She was married at the residence of her step-father, R. M. White, Esq., in Charlotte, N. C., October 14, 1879, by Rev. A. W. Miller, D.D., to Walter S. Pharr, son of the late Rev. Samuel Pharr, D.D., who was born in Mecklinburg County, N. C., July 10, 1856. Walter S. Pharr is an efficient member of the "Board of Education" of Mecklinburg County, N. C. They have five children, Robert Baxter, born October 22, 1880; Ernest Springs, January 4, 1883; Walter Hazel,

December 26, 1886; Edgar Walker, March 4, 1889; and Jennie Estelle, July 22, 1894.

Elizabeth Jane Walker's second marriage was to R. M. White, of Charlotte, N. C., which took place at her residence in Mecklinburg County, December 14, 1865. The fruit of this union was two children, John Wilson, born October 14, 1866; and William Cyrus, July 14, 1868. John Wilson was married to Anna Heilig Holmes, of Salisbury. N. C., October 20, 1891. One child was born to these parents, John Holmes, January 15, 1893. Anna Holmes White died January 28, 1893. The motherless grandchild and the two sons are all under the parental roof in Charlotte, N. C.

Eleanor Ann, youngest child of Hugh Harris by the second marriage, was born May 21, 1838, and was married to Hugh William Stinson, January 9, 1857. The fruit of this union was twelve children, only seven of whom are living, Elizabeth Jane, Cora Bethel, John Harris, Martha Rebecca, Mark Matthews, Ella, Julia, James Walker, Corinna Annice and McKamia Wilson. We failed to secure the names of the other two and have no dates of the father's death. The mother of these children died November 19, 1878.

Elizabeth Jane, the eldest child, married William Alexander. Seven children were born to these parents, Eleanor Mabel, Elizabeth Jane, Eugene, Edgar Walker, Maurise Stinson, Heriot Clarkson and Ida Manica.

Ella, sixth child of Eleanor and William Stinson, married John Dunlap, and they have two children, Eleanor and Maurise.

Corinna Annice, ninth child of Eleanor and William Stinson, married William Clark. They have two children, Eleanor and Eloise.

Jane Matthews Harris, widow of Hugh Harris, was married November 30, 1841, to Hon. John Walker, an elder in Sardis congregation. She died October 16, 1856, in her thirty-ninth year, and her remains rest in the cemetery at Sardis Church, Mecklinburg County, N. C.

Hugh Harris' remains lie in the cemetery at Providence Presbyterian Church. He lived and died in the bounds of that church.

Brown Lee, the youngest child of Robert and Jane McCaule Harris, married Mary Hart. They had one child, a daughter Sarah, who married J. J. Porter, of Providence, Mecklinburg County. Nine children are the fruit of this marriage, Rebecca, Edgar, Martha, Mary, Sarah, John, James, Annice and Banks.

Edgar, second child, married Miss Crenshaw.

Martha, third child, married Herbert Frost. They have two children, Ethel and Malinda.

John, sixth child, married Susan Leper.

Brown Lee's second marriage was to Mrs. Thompson. Mary Isabella is the only child of this marriage.

She married Simon M. Mills. Two children were born to these parents, Ladson Harris, deceased, and Cynthia Elizabeth, who married B. Frank Massey. Four children are the fruit of this union, John McCullough, Franklin, Ladson Mills and Leonidas.

Brown Lee remained in the home with his father, caring for him in his declining years.

This completes the record of the descendants of Robert Harris, second son of John and Eleanor Reynolds, so far as our information goes. From some of the families we failed to get any information, and others seem to be lost sight of altogether. This we very much regret. While none have entered the medical or legal professions, we find six in the ministry, Josiah Harris, James M. McKee, James Spratt, and John Stitt Harris, while James M. Walker and G. W. Davies are connected by marriage, all reared in the Presbyterian faith.

CHAPTER IX.

JOHN HARRIS, JR., THIRD SON OF JOHN AND ELEANOR REYNOLDS HARRIS, AND MARY GRIER, ELDEST CHILD OF JOHN HARRIS, JR.

John Harris, third son of John and Eleanor Reynolds Harris, was born in Lancaster County, Pa., in 1763. He was married in 1790, and as we have his marriage recorded by himself, one hundred and five years ago, will give it in his own words: "John Harris and Martha Hunter were joined in wedlock April 1, 1790."

Martha was a daughter of Robert and Mary Hunter, of Big Steele Creek Congregation, Mecklinburg County, N. C. John departed this life on Sabbath, the 26th of September, 1824, aged sixty-one years. Martha, his wife, died October 6, 1830, in the sixty-ninth year of her age. The remains of both lie in Big Steele Creek Cemetery, where all the older members of the Harris' family are interred, and in which church the father and sons once worshipped.

John settled on land adjoining his father's plantation, west of Lower Steele Creek, or "Blackstock Church." The old building of this church was removed several years ago, and nothing marks the place except the grave yard, which is enclosed with a neat rock wall, and contains the dust of some of the Harris' family in common with others. The congregation, desiring a more modern building and also a more central location, erected a church four miles north of the old church, on the public road leading from Charlotte, N. C., to Yorkville, S. C.

As was the custom with the early settlers, the dwelling was located near the spring. In a short time this building gave way to a more commodious dwelling farther up the slope, with a well of water in the yard, and every other improvement necessary to the convenience and comfort of a country home. In this home John and Martha Harris lived and died, and here all the marriage festivities of the children were held, of which there were five, viz., those of Mary, Eleanor, Nancy, John Moore and Martha Hunter. John Harris, Jr., was generally called "Capt." John Harris, having been an officer of the State Militia.

Mary, his eldest child, was born March 30, 1791, and married Colonel Thomas I. Grier, of Steele Creek, December 18, 1810. Colonel Grier was born December 25, 1785, and died April 10, 1872, aged eighty-seven years. Mary Grier died November 26, 1845, aged fifty-four years. The remains of both rest in the cemetery at Big Steele Creek Church.

Their children are eight in number: John Harris, James Alexander, Martha Hannah, Thomas Pringle, Ebenezer Clarkson, Mary Jane, Charles Strong and Anderson. John Harris, eldest child of Mary and Colonel Thomas I. Grier, was born September 25, 1811, and was married to Margaret P. Ross at the residence of Dr. John Moore Harris, her brother-in-law, York County, S. C., by Rev. Archibald White May 8, 1834. Margaret was born March 30, 1813, and died October 19, 1841. John Harris died May 12, 1864. They had two children, Malvina and William Lowndes. Malvina was born February 21, 1835, and died May 10, 1883, and lies by the side of her parents in Big Steele Creek Cemetery. Her first marriage was to James Blankenship, who soon died, leaving one child, Margaret Ella, who married James Harris October 19, 1871, a descendant of Robert Harris, Sr. Her second marriage was to James Elms, who fell a victim to the late war, leaving Malvina with two children, Eula and William A.

Eula married Frank Wiley, and died in 1891, leaving six children, Arthur, Eleanor, Bessie, Grier, Clara and Lillian. William A., second child of Malvina and James Elms, was married to Emma L. Garrison, of York County, S. C., January 11, 1888, by Rev. J. K. Fant. They have three children, Ella Gertrude, born October 16, 1888; Mary Lorenna, May 22, 1891, and Livy Grier, March 1, 1893.

William Lowndes, second child of John H. and Margaret P. Grier, was born May 10, 1838, and married Mary Barron, of York County, S. C., daughter of John Barron. Two sons were born to them, Frank Barron and Harry Percy. Both sons entered the "Legal Profession." William Lowndes' second marriage was to Fannie Kensey.

John Harris Grier's second marriage was to Mrs.

Emeline Bowden March 10, 1846. They had only one child, Frances Mary, who was born January 22, 1850. She married N. Wimble, of Virginia; one child was the fruit of this marriage, Mary Emeline. Fannie M. Wimble died October, 1891.

John Harris Grier's third marriage was to Lucy Smith, of York County, S. C., January 5, 1860, by whom he had two sons, Leonard and Thomas. Leonard was born November 12, 1860; Thomas J. May 10, 1863.

Leonard married Julia Gardy. Their children are Lorenna and Lucy. Leonard and Thomas are residents of Florida.

James Alexander Grier, second child of Mary and Thomas I. Grier, born September 14, 1814, was also married three times, first to Jane Moore, of York County, S. C., November 24, 1842, who died June 23, 1846.

The second marriage was to Jemima Crawford January 16, 1849. The children of this marriage are Henry Clay born March 7, 1853; William Baird, Mary Patton, Robert Lee, John Calvin, Leyden Tippoo, Charles Strong, Arthur Locke and James Alexander, all deceased.

Henry Clay married Anna Cochran. Their only children are twins. Roger and Russell. Jemima C. Grier died August 5, 1857.

James A. Grier's third marriage was to Mrs. Mary Ann Caruth, Oct. 20, 1858. The fruit of this marriage was twins, Hyden L. and Laura Anna, born Oct., 1867.

Laura Anna married J. F. McAlexander. Their

children are Leland Sandford, Guy Grier, Roland Ross and Anna Laura.

James A. Grier moved to Mississippi soon after his first marriage and settled permanently there. He died, September 12, 1878, aged sixty-four years. His last wife, Mary Ann, died June 1st, 1879. His remains, with those of the deceased members of his family lie in Northern Mississippi, near to Holly Springs.

Martha Hannah, third child of Mary and Thos. I. Grier, was born November 28, 1817 and died in her father's house after a lingering illness on March 21, 1861, at the age of forty-four.

Thomas Pringle, fourth child, was born December 27, 1819, sought his fortune in the West at the time the "gold fever" first prevailed, but after a few years returned and entered into the mercantile business near the home of his childhood, where he died, August 28, 1859, at the age of forty years.

Ebenezer Clarkson, fifth child, was born December 11, 1821, graduated at the University of North Carolina at Chapel Hill, entered the legal profession, and settled in Macon, Ga., where he practiced his profession. He died May 30, 1888 at the age of sixty-seven.

Clarkson was twice married, first to Frances M. Poe of Georgia, November 3, 1854, by whom one child was born, Mary S., November 3, 1855, and married Thos. P. Ross, October 9, 1889.

Clarkson Grier's second marriage was to Mrs. Eliza T. Dorsey of Macon, Ga., October 18, 1859. The children of this marriage are Clark, born August

11, 1860; Fannie, January 12, 1862; Thomas, October, 1864; and Ross, January, 1866.

Clark, the eldest child of Clarkson and Eliza Grier, married Miss Waltham. Lois is their only child.

Fannie married Joseph Cook of Atlanta, Ga., December, 1887. Joseph and T. Griswold, are Fannie's children. Fannie Grier Cook died November 16, 1892.

Thomas, third child, married Fannie Christian.

Ross, fourth child, married Bessie Martin.

Mary Jane, sixth child of Mary and Thomas I. Grier, was born May 8, 1826, and married Robert A. Ross of Steele Creek, November 8, 1848 at the residence of her father, Rev. James B. Watt, officiating. Robert A. Ross was born July 12, 1821. He was a victim of the late war. Coming home in a reduced state of health, he died of typhoid pneumonia in the bosom of his family, January 24, 1863.

Mary Jane was left with five children, viz: Alice E., born November 12, 1849; Mary Martha, February 29, 1852; Thomas Pringle, December 12, 1854; William Alexander, born February 11, 1857, and died October, 19, 1857; James Herndon, March 25, 1859, and Charles Ellis, June 30, 1861.

Thomas Pringle, third child of Mary Jane, is a train conductor in the employ of the Southern Railway Company. He married Mary S. Grier, October 9, 1889, of the same branch of the Harris family with himself, daughter of the late Ebenezer Clarkson Grier of Macon, Ga. Their children are Robert Clarkson and Frances Shirley, twins, born November 4, 1891, and Eleanor Reynolds, born August 28, 1894 and died April 5, 1895.

James Herndon, fifth child of Mary Jane Ross, married Cora L. Smith, December 14, 1886, daughter of the late Captain Smith of Pineville, N. C., Rev. Charles E. McDonald, officiating. James H. is an elder in the Associate Reformed Presbyterian Church, Charlotte, N. C. Their children are Lloyd M., born December 3, 1888, an infant daughter born March 5, 1891. and died April 3, 1891, and Mary Dunn, born October 18, 1894.

Charles Ellis, sixth child of Mary Jane Ross, entered the medical profession, graduating from Maryland University, Baltimore. He is Assistant Physician in the State Branch Hospital for insane at Morganton, N. C. He married Kate Lenoir Chambers of Morganton, June 16, 1891. They have two children, Catharine Adalaide, born March 16, 1893, and Martha Grier, October 18, 1894.

Charles Strong, seventh child of Mary and Thomas I. Grier, was born June, 6, 1828. After the death of his father, he made his home with his brother James A. Grier, in Mississippi, and died there May 26, 1877, in the forty-ninth year of his age. Anderson, the youngest and eighth child, died in childhood.

Eleanor, second child of John and Martha Harris, was born October 14, 1792, married Hugh Harris, son of Hugh Harris, Senior. Her children are given under their father's name.

CHAPTER X.

NANCY HARRIS STRONG, THIRD CHILD OF JOHN HARRIS, JR., AND HER CHILDREN, DR. JOHN MASON STRONG, MARTHA JANE YOUNG AND MARY LETITIA CHALMERS.

Nancy, third child of John and Martha **Harris**, was also called Agnes, especially by her father. The two names were used interchangeably. The date of her birth is written in her father's own hand and she is called Agnes. We infer from this that she was baptised Agnes. He had her silver also all engraved "A. H."

Nancy or Agnes married Rev. Charles Strong of the Associate Reformed Church. Charles was a son of James and Letitia Strong of Chester District, S. C. Charles Strong was born August 4, 1788. Nancy Harris was born November 11, 1794. They were married February 13, 1817.

On January 10, 1805, the doors of the South Carolina College were opened for the first time, and Charles Strong entered with the first class the same year and graduated in 1808 in a class of thirty-one. He, with two others, Revs. James and Joseph Lowry, cousins of his own, furnished their own provision and boarded themselves in a room in the college building set apart for that purpose.

Judge O'Neall of South Carolina, once a devoted pupil of Charles Strong and also his biographer, says: "Notwithstanding this difficulty, by which many of the present youths would not only be startled, but would be turned back from the pursuit of an education, these clever young men pursued their studies, graduated good scholars and became useful men. And all afterwards became ministers of the Gospel, teachers and preachers of their mighty Master's word." After graduating Charles Strong taught the Newberry Academy with ability and success for several years.

In the Autumn of 1811 he was received as a student of theology by the First Presbytery of the Carolinas. Soon after he entered the Associate Reformed Seminary in New York City, and took a four years course of theology under Dr. John M. Mason, D. D.

He was licensed July 13, 1815. Accepting a call from the united congregations of Cannon's Creek, King's Creek and Prosperity, in Newberry District, S. C., he was ordained to the office of the holy ministry, and on the 8th of November, 1816, was installed pastor of these congregations. Here he labored with much acceptance for the short period of eight years, when he was stricken down with a malignant fever which closed his earthly labors in the vigor of his days, and in the midst of great usefulness, on Tuesday the 20th of July, 1824. Charles Strong was also the founder of the Newberry Auxiliary Bible Society and its President until his death. His remains lie in the cemetery at Cannon's Creek Church.

The following is a copy of the inscription upon his monument.

> " Sacred
> To the memory of the Rev. Charles Strong,
> Son of James Strong Esq. of
> Chester District, and
> pastor for eight years of the Congregations
> of King's Creek, Cannon's Creek
> and Prosperity.
> He lived beloved, and died lamented
> by all who knew him. On the 20th
> of July 1824, in the 36th year of his age,
> his life of usefulness closed.
> He was distinguished for his vigorous
> intellect and amiable manners,
> his unassuming and dignified de-
> portment, his solid and extensive
> learning, his firm attachment
> to Evangelical truth, his fervent
> and consistent piety.
>
> ' Mark the perfect man and behold
> the upright, for the end of that
> man is peace.' "

The grave is enclosed and covered with a neat marble slab, the loving tribute of devoted parishioners. Five children were left fatherless by his death, John Mason, Martha Jane, Mary Letitia, Eleanor Euphemia and Nancy Caroline. In two short months the young mother experienced another bereavement in the death of her father, John Harris, Jr., upon whom she leaned for earthly comfort and support. But in those short months he was not unmindful of her comfort, as he had provided for her a comfortable home near to his own, in Steele Creek, N. C., where she removed and spent her remaining days. She died November 8, 1842, in her forty-eight year.

Her only son, John Mason, was born in Newberry County, S. C., September 1, 1818, and entered Jefferson College in Cannonsburg, Pa., in 1839, and graduated in 1841, under the presidency of Dr. Matthew Brown. He chose the medical profession and attended one course of lectures in Charleston, S. C., but graduated from the Jefferson Medical College, Philadelphia, Pa., in 1847. His first and only home has been in Steele Creek, where he was reared, and there he has successfully practiced his profession for nearly fifty years, attaining an eminence and popularity reached by only a favored few. He is a ruling elder in Steele Creek Associate Reformed Church.

John Mason has been twice married, first to Rachel Eleanor Harris, daughter of Dr. John Moore Harris, on April 7, 1851. Their children are Elva Euphemia, Charles Moore, Lola May, William Mason and Egbert Hill, who was born June 12, 1865, and died July 8, 1866, aged one year.

Elva Euphemia was born August 31, 1852, married John Miller Boyce, of York County, S. C., December 20, 1870, a son of Wm. Boyce. J. M. Boyce was born November 23, 1848, and pursued an eclectic course in Erskine College for two years. The fruit of this marriage was one son, John Mason, born September 4, 1879. John M. Boyce died July 22, 1879. His remains lie in Blackstock Cemetery.

Elva Euphemia's second marriage was to W. Frank Moore, of York County, S. C., February, 1884. They have one son, Oren McCreight, born May 31, 1886. Their home is in Blacksburg, York County, S. C.

Charles Moore, second child of Dr. J. M. Strong, entered the medical profession, located near his father in Steele Creek, and is associated with him in his practice. Charles Moore graduated from the University of Maryland after a three year's course in 1887. In 1891 he took a post graduate course in the Polyclinic School in New York City. He married Kate Ross Miller April 21, 1891, a descendant of Robert Harris, Sr. Charles Moore was born September 19, 1862; Kate Ross, November 17, 1870. She is a graduate of the Due West Female College of the class of 1890. Charles Miller is their only child, born February 27, 1892.

Lola May, third child of Dr. J. M. and Rachel Eleanor Strong, was born December 29, 1867. She was married at her father's residence in 1890 by Rev. C. E. McDonald to Edgar Harris Peoples, a descendant of Hugh Harris, Sr. She has one child mentioned under its father's name.

William Mason, the youngest child of Dr. J. M. Strong, was born September 22, 1875. Rachel Eleanor, the mother of these children, was born July 27, 1832, and died May 27, 1880. Her remains lie in the cemetery at Big Steele Creek Church. Dr. John Mason Strong's second marriage was to Mrs. Nancy Grier, at her residence in Steele Creek, September 5, 1883, Rev. Charles E. McDonald performing the ceremony.

Martha Jane, second child of Rev. Charles and Nancy Strong, was born in Newberry County, S. C., January 18, 1820. She was married at the residence of her mother, in Steele Creek, N. C., by Rev. Isaac Grier, D. D., to Rev. John S. Pressly, of the Associate Reformed Church, September 29, 1842. Rev. John S. Pressly graduated from the South Carolina College. In 1831 he was a member of the Legislature of South Carolina, and it is a matter of history, that partly through his influence and measures introduced by him into the House of Representatives, steps were taken that led to the impeachment and removal of the learned, but infidel, President of South Carolina College, Dr. Cooper. John S. Pressly was for some years before he entered the ministry a popular educator. He was the founder of the Academy at Due West, S. C., that developed into Erskine College in 1839.

His first theological course was taken at Oxford, O., under the presidency of Rev. Joseph Claybaugh, D. D. The second year was in the Seminary at Allegheny, Pa., under the presidency of Rev. John T. Pressly, D.D. He was licensed October 8, 1840, at Bethel, Lincoln County, Tenn., by the Second Presbytery of the Synod of the South, and was ordained by the same Presbytery, at a meeting of Synod at Coddle Creek, N. C., October 14, 1841. He accepted a call from the congregations of Bethel and Ebenezer, in Burke and Jefferson Counties, Ga., in 1842. In April 1843 he was installed pastor by the Georgia Presbytery. Rev. John S. Pressly was forced from ill-health to resign his charge in 1847. He then located near to Generostee Church, Anderson County, S. C., teaching and preaching as he was able. His long and useful life came to a close June 1, 1863. His remains repose in the cemetery of Generostee Church, Anderson County, S. C.

Martha Jane's second marriage was to Rev. James L. Young, of the Associate Reformed Church, January 8, 1867. Mr. Young, a son of Francis Young and brother of Rev. J. N. Young, LL. D., was born in Abbeville County, S. C., December 8, 1808. He graduated in the Miami University, Oxford, O. His theological course was taken in the Associate Reformed Seminary in Allegheny, Pa., under the presidency of Rev. John T. Pressly, D. D. In 1836 he was ordained by the Second Presbytery, and installed pastor over the united congregations of Bethel, Laurensville, Providence and Head Spring, Laurens County, S. C. He demitted this charge in 1851, and removed to Pontotoc County, Miss., and organized Bethany congregation, and in 1853 was installed by the Memphis Presbytery of the "Synod of the South," over Bethany and Hopewell Churches, Miss. Here Rev. James L. Young spent the remainder of his useful life, until terminated by a severe attack of pneumonia on the 31st of January, 1867. His remains lie in the cemetery at Bethany Church, Miss.

After the death of Rev. J. S. Pressly, Martha Jane made her home in the family of Rev. J. N. Young, LL. D., her brother-in-law, taking care of his eight motherless children. In this home her second marriage took place to Rev. J. L. Young, after whose death, she returned to Rev. J. N. Young's and remained until his death. She now makes her home with his youngest daughter, Harriet, who married James E. Todd, of Due West, S. C.

Mary Letitia, third child of Rev. Charles and Nancy Strong, was born in Newberry County, S. C., April 12, 1821. She was married on the 12th of December, 1839, by Rev. Isaac Grier, D. D., at the residence of her mother in Steele Creek, N. C., to Rev. James Clark Chalmers, of the Associate Reformed Church, son of Captain James Chalmers of Newberry County, S. C. James Clark Chalmers, was born April 11, 1811. His academical course was under the Rev. Samuel P. Pressly, his pastor, at the Newberry Academy. He entered Franklin College, Athens, Georgia, in 1834, and graduated in August, 1836, under the Presidency of Rev. A. Church, D. D. He was a graduate of the first-class of students in the Theological Seminary of the Associate Reformed Church, located at Due West, S. C., under the Presidency of Rev, E. E. Pressly, D. D. On October 5, 1838, he was licensed by the Second Presbytery of the Associate Reformed Synod of the South, at Providence Church, Laurens County, S. C. In the same year he accepted a call from the united congregations of Generostee, Shiloh and Midway in Anderson County, S. C., was ordained at a meeting of the Presbytery at Bethel Church, Georgia, in April, 1840, and in May of the same year was installed pastor of these churches. Here he labored for nineteen years, with the exception of two or three interruptions by order of Synod. In the fall of 1844, he was directed by Synod to spend four months in South Georgia and Middle Florida, and while there he re-organized the church of Pleasant Grove, in Decatur County, Georgia. For several months during the years 1854 and 1855, he was engaged as agent for the endowment of Erskine College. Again, from October, 1856, till October 1857, he labored in a mission church in the City of Nashville, Tenn. In 1858 he accepted a call from Steele Creek, Mecklinburg County, N. C., and Blackstock, York County, S. C., and on the last Friday of October of the same year was installed pastor of this charge. In this field he faithfully labored, though often in extreme physical suffering, till 1882, when he was forced from continued ill-health to resign. He died at the residence of his son, Rev. John T. Chalmers, in Winnsboro, S. C., on Thursday morning, July 7, 1887, in the seventy-seventh year of his age and forty-ninth of his ministry. His remains repose in the cemetery of the Associate Reformed Church in Winnsboro, S. C.

Rev. J. C. and M. L. Chalmers had nine children, Charles Strong, born January 6, 1842; Nancy Priscilla, January 10, 1844; a son, September 15, 1845; a son, July 14, 1847; Mary Jane, September 17, 1848; Caroline, April 5, 1851; a daughter, August 12, 1853; a son, April 29, 1858, and John Thomas, June 6, 1860. All died in infancy, except the youngest, and their mortal remains sleep together in Generostee burial ground, the first grave ever opened in that cemetery being a bed for the first born.

Of this sore bereavement Rev. Dr. Lathan, in a memorial sketch of Rev. J. C. Chalmers, says: "No pen can describe how sore the hearts of these parents were made. Sore for life, but with Christian meekness they said, "the Lord gave and the Lord hath taken away, blessed be the name of the Lord." These sore bereavements were overruled for good to Mr. Chalmers. They prepared him to enter the chamber of distress and comfort those whose hearts were bleeding as those ministers who have not passed through like afflictions can not do."

In 1849 these parents took charge of Lewis M. McAlister, an infant son of L. W. and Matilda Pressly McAlister, whose mother had recently died. They raised him as their own son, and he owns and occupies the Chalmers home place in Steele Creek, and with him M. L. Chalmers makes her home at present, since her son's removal to Philadelphia. He is an elder and Superintendent of the Sabbath-school at Central Steele Creek, and chairman of the County Board of Education, Mecklinburg County, N. C. He was born in Lowndesville, Abbeville County, S. C. December 13, 1848. On November 21, 1870 he married M. Addie Whisonant of York County, S. C. They have four children. Calvin Wardlaw, born in North Carolina, August 31, 1871; Mary Isabella, in South Carolina, January 17, 1875; Gertrude, in North Carolina, November, 7, 1876, and L. Melville, December 12,

1883. His father, L. W. McAlister was an honored elder in Generostee Church, South Carolina.

John Thomas, youngest and only surviving child of Jas. C. and Mary L. Chalmers, was born in Mecklinburg County, N. C., June 6, 1860. At the age of thirteen he made a public profession of religion, entered Erskine College at fifteen and graduated in 1878, sharing the honors of the class. His theological studies were pursued first under the direction of his father, then at Erskine Seminary, South Carolina, and Union Theological Seminary, New York City.

Later he took a special course in Hebrew under Professor W. R. Harper, President of Chicago University. He was licensed April 6, 1880, at Steele Creek, N. C., the church of his childhood and spiritual birth, by the First Presbytery of the Associate Reformed Presbyterian Church, South. Before leaving Union Seminary, he received calls from New York City, North and South Carolina. Accepting the one from South Carolina, he was ordained and installed pastor at Winnsboro, S. C., April 28, 1881, his venerable father presiding in the exercises of the occasion. The happy relation formed between pastor and people continued for nearly eleven years, and was only terminated when the pastor, under a strong sense of duty, accepted a call from the Fourth United Presbyterian Church of Philadelphia. During his Winnsboro pastorate the membership more than doubled itself. During five years of this period he was associated with Rev. W. M. Grier, D. D., in the editorial conduct of the *Associate Reformed Presbyterian*, the denominational organ, and contributed more than six hundred articles to its columns. Three months in the year 1884, he spent as a special agent for Erskine Theological Seminary, raising an additional endowment of $25,000.

On October 26, 1882, John T. Chalmers was married to Johnnie Caroline Brice, of Fairfield County, S. C., by Rev. R. G. Miller, assisted by Rev. J. C. Chalmers. She was a daughter of John and Agnes C. Brice, and a descendant of the same branch of the Harris family, a woman whose sweetness of disposition and amiability of manner rendered her deservedly popular and successful as a pastor's wife, and who contributed in no small measure to her husband's success. She was born October 18, 1863, and died on Sabbath morning, January 15, 1893. These parents have six children, Eva, born November 8, 1883; Mary Agnes, February 4, 1885; Palmer, November 26, 1886; Charles Brice, August 14, 1888, and died March 7, 1889; John Thomas, July 20, 1890, and died January 11, 1893, just three days before his mother's death; and James Cuyler, born in Philadelphia, Pa., February 2, 1892.

In October, 1891, Jno. T. Chalmers became pastor of the Fourth United Presbyterian Church of Philadelphia, where he continues to labor. This congregation is the largest of the *twelve* U. P. Churches of the city, and one of the six largest in the body. In May 1892, he started a mission school with eleven scholars. In *three years* he has seen this enterprise develop into a church with fifty members, a pastor of its own, and a Sabbath-school of two hundred and seventy-five. It is known as the Wharton Square United Presbyterian Church.

CHAPTER XI.

ELEANOR EUPHEMIA YOUNG AND NANCY CAROLINE PATTERSON, YOUNGEST CHILDREN OF NANCY HARRIS STRONG.

Eleanor Euphemia, fourth child of Rev. Charles and Nancy Strong, was born in Newberry County, S. C., January 19, 1823, and died October 28, 1862, in her thirty-ninth year. She was married to Rev. John N. Young, then Professor in Erskine College, by Rev. James Clark Chalmers, at his home in Anderson County, S. C., on Tuesday morning, October 21, 1845.

Rev. John N. Young, a son of Francis Young, of Abbeville County, S. C., was born February 17, 1813. He entered Miami University, Oxford, Ohio, in 1833, and graduated under the presidency of Dr. Bishop, August 10, 1837. He was taken under the care of the Second Presbytery of the Synod of the South the same year, and while prosecuting his theological studies at Due West, he was also employed in teaching mathematics in the High School at the same place, which in 1839 assumed the features of a regularly chartered and equipped college. In this college he was elected Professor of Mathematics, which position he held till 1881, when his resignation was accepted at a meeting of the Synod in Bethel Church, Alabama. He was licensed, and probably ordained at the same time, at a meeting of the Second Presbytery at Bethel, Lincoln County, Tenn., October 8, 1840. His long and useful life was spent in Due West, S. C., having been professor forty-two years in Erskine College. He was also treasurer of the college for nearly the same period of time.

In June, 1891, the Board of Trustees of Erskine College conferred the degree of LL. D., on Professor Young. In addition to his scholarly attainments, he was the personification of meekness, patience and submission under all the trials that came to him in the positions that he filled, and was universally admired for his gentle, lovable disposition. About two weeks before his death he sustained a serious injury from a fall that so shocked his system that death resulted October 31, 1891, in the seventy-ninth year of his age. His remains lie in the cemetery at Due West, S. C.

Rev. John N. and E. Euphemia Young were the parents of ten children, viz., Elizabeth Jane, Charles Strong, M. Henry Martin, John Mason, James Little, Nancy Caroline, Mary Evelyn, Eleanor Euphemia, Martha Anna and Harriet.

Elizabeth Jane, the first child of Rev. J. N. and E. Euphemia Young, was born at Due West July 8, 1846. She graduated from the Female College at Due West in 1862, was married by Rev. Robert C. Grier, D. D., May 17, 1870, to Rev. Ebenezer Pressly McClintock, of the Associate Reformed Presbyterian Church, a son of John and Mary McClintock, of Laurens County, S. C., and born June 11, 1845. His paternal grandmother was Jane Law, his maternal grandmother a Martin.

He graduated from Erskine College, Due West, in 1861. A few months after graduating he entered the Confederate service, serving during 1863 and 1864 in Company S, Second South Carolina Cavalry, Hampton's Brigade. His theological course was in the Seminary at Due West, S. C. Graduating in 1869, he was licensed August 22, 1869, at Prosperity, Newberry County, S. C., by the Second Presbytery of the "Synod of the South." After his licensure, E. P. McClintock supplied the churches in Mississippi, Tennessee, Kentucky, and Newberry County, S. C., for more than a year. Accepting a call from King's Creek, Newberry County, and Thompson Street Church, Newberry Village, S. C., he was ordained and installed over these churches by the Second Presbytery August 12, 1871. He labored as pastor of these churches until September, 1883, when he demitted King's Creek. Since that date he has devoted all of his time to Thompson Street Church. His home is in the town of Newberry, S. C.

Five children were born to Rev. E. P. and Elizabeth J. McClintock, only two of whom lived beyond infancy, Euphemia and Mary Law. Euphemia graduated from the "Woman's College," Baltimore, Md., in 1893, and since that date has been engaged in teaching in her native town. Mary Law also graduated from the same college at the close of the term, June, 1895.

Charles Strong, second child of Eleanor E. and Rev. John N. Young, was born at Due West, S. C., July 5, 1847; graduated from Erskine College, in 1869, and from Erskine Theological Seminary in 1871. Was licensed by the Second Presbytery of the Associate Reformed Church, at King's Creek, Newberry County, S. C., August 11, 1871. Accepting a call from Head Spring Congregation, Tenn., he was installed pastor of that church by the Tennessee Presbytery, May 2, 1873. Charles Strong Young spent the year 1882 in mission work in the city of Louisville, Ky. In 1884 the pastoral relation between himself and Head Spring was dissolved. He then removed to Florida, and organized a church, Arlington, Fla., in 1888, one at Orleans, in 1889, and another in Bartow, Fla., in 1890. He has been pastor of the two first named churches since their organization. His home is near Orleans Church, Citrus County, Fla.

He was married by Rev. E. P. McClintock, to May B. Chalmers, of Newberry, S. C., September 26, 1871, daughter of the late William Chalmers, of Newberry, S. C. May B. Chalmers is a graduate of the Due West Female College, of the class 1867.

The fruit of this marriage is six children. The eldest, an infant son, born April 7, died April 15, 1873; John Mason, born September 26, 1874; Elizabeth Caroline, August 10, 1877; Jane Strong, February 3, 1879; Charles Henry, August 6, 1881, and William Chalmers, born in Citrus County, Fla., April 17, 1889.

Elizabeth Caroline, third child of Rev. Charles S. and May B. Young, was married at the residence of her father, in Citrus County, Fla., by Rev. D. G. Philips, Jr., of Bartow, Fla., to James Taylor McDill, of Due West, September 7, 1894.

M. Henry Martin, third child of Eleanor E. and Rev. J. N. Young, was born in Due West, S. C., October 16, 1848.

He graduated from Erskine College in 1869 in the class with his brother, Rev. Charles S. Young. He went into the mercantile business, and is a citizen of Due West, and deacon in the Associate Reformed Church of that place. Henry Martin occupies his father's home, "The Young Residence." He was married by Rev. D. F. Haddon in 1872, to Flora Josephine Todd, at the residence of her father, in Laurens, S. C., a daughter of the late James Todd. She was born in Laurens County, S. C., March 4, 1852, and is a graduate of the Due West Female College, of the class of 1870.

These parents have eight children; Jane McClintock, born November 25, 1873, and a graduate of the Female College at Due West; John Todd, born October 16, 1876; Euphemia Strong, September 4, 1879; James Rogers, April 2, 1882; Charles Henry, September 7, 1884; Mason Pressly, June 26, 1886; Flora Lois, January 5, 1889, and Edwin Reynolds, September 16, 1892.

John Mason, fourth child of Eleanor E. and Rev. J. N. Young, was born in Due West, S. C., July 29, 1850, graduated from Erskine College in 1870, and entered the legal profession. Locating in Covington, Tenn., he practiced his profession until January, 1889, when he removed to Citrus County, Fla., and is located in Invernes. John Mason has been twice married, first to Sophronia O. Howard, at Tabernacle, Tenn., June 11, 1879, by Rev. Samuel D. Boggs, of the Presbyterian Church. The fruit of this union was two children, Charles Pressly, born in Covington, Tenn., March 20, 1880, and died December 17, 1880; and Elizabeth, born April 11, 1881. Sophronia Howard Young died in Covington, Tenn., October 9, 1881.

John Mason's second marriage was to Mrs. Anna S. Jones, of Mississippi, June 15, 1886, by Rev. Bowden, an Episcopal minister. The fruit of this marriage was three children, John Mason, born in Covington, Tenn., July 31, 1887; Ernest Taylor, born in Orleans, Fla., November 14, 1889, and Anna May, born in Orleans, Fla., February 25, 1892, and died August 1, 1893.

James Little Young, fifth child of Rev. J. N. and E. Euphemia Young, was born at Due West, S. C., January 19, 1852. He graduated from Erskine College, Due West, S. C., July 12, 1871. The same year he entered the Theological Seminary at Due West, and graduated July, 1873. He also spent the following winter in the Seminary, and was licensed by the Second Presbytery of the Synod of the South, at Generostee Church, Anderson County, S. C., September 6, 1873. By order of Synod he spent the year 1874 among the churches of Texas. The year 1875 was spent supplying the churches in Arkansas. Returning to South Carolina he was ordained at Due West by the Second Presbytery, October 30, 1875. During the years 1876 and 1877 he supplied Mount Zion Church, Missouri. He also labored in Tennessee during the year 1878.

Returning to Arkansas he accepted a call from the churches, Monticello and Saline, Arkansas, and was installed by the Arkansas Presbytery at Monticello, April 23, 1881, the late Rev. John Wilson conducting the exercises, assisted by Rev. J. S. A. Hunter, now missionary in Mexico. He was installed at Saline Church, April 3, 1881.

Rev. James L. Young was married to Jennie Bonner Young at the residence of Samuel Brice, near Harrals, Dallas County, Ala., by Rev. James A. Lowry, assisted by Rev. Charles S. Young. She is the daughter of the late Rev. James M. Young of Alabama, and was born in Dallas County, Ala., October 17, 1858. The issue of this marriage is five children, viz: Euphemia Jane, born September 30, 1884; James Ulric, January 15, 1886; Mary Hunter, October 24, 1887; Flora Craig, April 17, 1889, and Kate Strong, December, 10, 1890.

It is an interesting fact that the two eldest of these children, Euphemia Jane and James Ulric, were admitted to the communion of the church during a meeting in September, 1894 at their father's church at Monticello, Ark., at the tender age of ten and eight years respectively.

Nancy Caroline, sixth child of Rev. J. N. and E. Euphemia Young, was born December 27, 1853, and when a sweet little girl of six years, was drowned in a cistern, in her father's garden, June 14, 1859.

Mary Evelyn, seventh child of Rev. J. N. and E. Euphemia Young, was born at Due West, S. C., September 14th, 1855, graduated from the Female College at Due West, 1873, and was married at her father's residence in Due West, October 4, 1881, to Rev. H. McMaster Henry, of the Associate Reformed Church, son of the late Captain Henry of Chester, S. C. H. M. Henry, was born in Chester County, S. C., December 9, 1852, graduated from Erskine College, Due West, S. C., July, 1872, from the Theological Seminary of the same place 1876, was licensed by the Second Presbytery of the "Synod of the South," September 20, 1876, was ordained by the same Presbytery September 28, 1878, and accepting a call from Bethel Church, Ala., was installed pastor of that church by the Tennessee and Alabama Presbytery in the autumn of 1879. He is located at Allenton, Ala.

Rev. H. McMaster and Mary Evelyn Henry, have five children, Jonathan Edwards, born July 30, 1882; Euphemia Strong, May 3, 1884; Sarah Torbit, February 28, 1887; William John, August 28, 1889; and Jamie Bonner, October 25, 1892.

Eleanor Euphemia, eighth child of Eleanor E. and Rev. J. N. Young, was born February 8, 1857, and died, May 13, 1858, aged, one year and three months.

Martha Anna, ninth child of Eleanor E. and Rev. J. N. Young, was born in Due West, December 28, 1858. She is a graduate of the Female College, Due West, S. C., and for six years after her graduation was engaged in the College as Art Teacher. She was married at the residence of Hon. James E. Todd, her brother-in-law, near Due West, S. C., by Rev. Charles S. Young of Orleans, Fla., assisted by Rev. E. P. McClintock and Dr. W. M. Grier, October, 1892, to Rev. J. E. Johnson, of the Associate Reformed Church. Rev. J. E. Johnson is a native of the North, born perhaps in the State of Ohio. He came South as a student of theology from the United Presbyterian Church. His literary education having been completed, he connected with the Second Presbytery of the Synod of the South and entered the Theological Seminary at Due West, S. C., graduating after a full course in 1891. He was licensed and ordained by the Second Presbytery, and for eighteen months supplied the Mission Church in Atlanta, Ga. On account of throat trouble he spent sometime in Pasedena, Cal., but is now located at Covington, Ala. They have two children, Eleanor Bourland, and a son, born May 23, 1895.

Harriet, tenth child of Eleanor E. and Rev. J. N. Young, was born in Due West, September 19, 1861. She graduated from the Due West Female College in 1880, and was married at her father's residence June 2, 1885, by Rev. Wm. L. Pressly, D. D., to James E. Todd, of Due West, son of the Late James Todd. James E. Todd was born in Laurens County, S. C., January 17, 1853, and is connected with the "Harris family," by a former marriage to Jane E. H. Grier, daughter of Rev. R. C. Grier, D. D., and a descendant of the Hugh Harris Sr. branch. Their home is near Due West, S. C. They have three children, John Young, born January 17, 1888, Elizabeth Jane, October 1, 1889; and James Rogers, November 20, 1891.

Nancy Caroline, fifth child of Rev. Charles and Nancy Strong, was born April 3, 1824. She was only three months old at the death of her father. On January 29, 1845, she was married by Rev. John S. Pressly at his residence in Burke County, Georgia, to Augustine Little Patterson, of Burke County, Ga. Two children were the fruit of this marriage, Nancy Eugenia, born November 19, 1845, and an infant son, who died, August 26, 1847. Nancy Caroline died August 31, 1847, aged twenty-three years and five months.

Nancy Eugenia, the eldest child of Augustine and Nancy C. Patterson, married James B. Dawson of Burke County, Ga. She too had a short married life. Her only child preceded her to the grave. A severe cold brought on a serious bronchial and lung trouble, which closed her precious life, after weeks of great prostration, on April 2, 1870, aged twenty-four years and five months, thus closing forever the earthly record of this branch of the Nancy Harris Strong family. The dust of this family sleeps in Bethel cemetery, Ga.

Augustine, L. Patterson was married the second time to Eleanor Edgeworth, of Americus, Ga., by whom he had three daughters and one son. Only two of the children survive.

This closes the record of the descendants of Nancy Harris Strong, daughter of John Harris, Jr., and granddaughter of John and Eleanor Reynolds Harris.

CHAPTER XII.

DR. JOHN MOORE HARRIS AND MARTHA HARRIS STRONG, YOUNGEST CHILDREN OF JOHN HARRIS, JR.

John Moore, only son and fourth child of Captain John and Martha Harris, was born in York County, S. C., on Friday, February 3, 1797. He graduated from "South Carolina College," December, 1819. He chose the medical profession, and entered upon a full course in the medical schools of New York City and Philadelphia, graduating in 1822.

On Tuesday, April 19, 1825, he was married to Evelina Eliza Ross. He located near to the place of his birth, on land adjoining his father. He had an extensive practice, rose to eminence in his profession and was endowed with both mental and physical ability, but in the midst of his usefulness was seized with a violent attack of pneumonia, which in a few days ended his life. He died March 20, 1848, in the fifty-first year of his age. Evelina Eliza Harris died July 19, 1855, aged fifty-three years. Their remains lie in the cemetery at Big Steele Creek Church.

These parents had six children, of whom only two are living, Frances C. Harris and Lorenna E. Pressly.

Malvina Desdemona, eldest child of Dr. John

Moore and Evelina E. Harris, was born January 12, 1828, and died January 9, 1833.

John Alexander, second child, was born August 27, 1830, and died March 16, 1839.

Laura Louisa Malvina, third child, was born August 27, 1835, and died March 5, 1836.

Rachael Eleanor, fourth child, was born July 27, 1832, married Dr. John M. Strong, April 7, 1851, and died May 27, 1880. Her children are given under their father's name.

Francis Calhoun, fifth child of Dr. John Moore and Evelina E. Harris, was born April 21, 1838. He spent a part of two years in Erskine College, and married Frances Isabella Barron, daughter of John Barron, of York County, S. C., January 4, 1859, the ceremony being performed by Rev. William B. Pressly. Francis C. Harris fills the office of deacon in Steele Creek Church, Rev. R. Livy Grier, pastor. The home of these parents is at Pineville, N. C. The following are their children: Eva Moore, born December 22, 1859; Ciprianna Pressly, June 23, 1861; Robert Ross, July 22, 1864; Eliza Eleanor, February 11, 1868; May Lorenna, May 31, 1871; Jane Hill, October 31, 1873; Albert Barron, June 22, 1875, and died May 24, 1880, aged four years and eleven months, and Frances Malvina, born April 16, 1880, and died July 11, 1881, aged fifteen months.

Eva Moore, eldest child of Francis C. and Frances Isabella Harris, was married at the residence of her parents December 18, 1879, to Oscar W. Potts, by Rev.

James C. Chalmers. Their children are, Alice Louise, born November 28, 1880, and died May 18, 1882, and Frank Glenn, born May 10, 1885.

Ciprianna Pressly, second child of Francis C. and Frances Isabella Harris, was married at the residence of her parents near Pineville to J. W. Hennegan, October 14, 1881, by Rev. G. Spring Robison. Their children are James Harris, born September 21, 1882; **Fred.** Barron, March 2, 1886; Frances Louise, May 30, 1889; Margaret Lee, May 7, 1892, and Leon Reynolds, born September 29, 1894.

Robert Ross, third child of Francis C. and Frances Isabella Harris, married Minnie Hester Blankenship, daughter of Dr. Blankenship, of York County, S. C., August 6, 1884. Minnie H. is a descendant of the Robert Harris branch. She died at her home in Pineville, N. C. Robert R. and Minnie H. Harris' children are Ellen Clair, born October 12, 1886, and Albert Grady, born July 2, 1888.

Lorenna Evelina, sixth child of Dr. John Moore and Evelina Harris, was born November 22, 1840. She was married to Rev. William Barron Pressly May 26, 1858, at the residence of Dr. John Mason Strong, her brother-in-law, in Mecklinburg County, N. C., by Rev. J. B. Watt. William B. Pressly, son of the late Richard Pressly, Esq., of York County, S. C., was born March 2, 1828. He graduated at Erskine College, Due West, S. C., July, 1849. After a full course in the Theological Seminary of the Associate Reformed Church at Due West, he was licensed by the First

Presbytery of the Synod of the Associate Reformed Church December, 1852, and ordained by the same Presbytery October, 1854. Accepting a call from New Sterling congregation, Iredell County, N. C., he was installed pastor of that congregation November 9, 1855. After serving this congregation for twenty-one years he demitted and accepted a call from the congregation in Statesville, Iredell County, N. C., and was installed pastor in 1876. Here he labored until his useful life came suddenly to a close by heart disease on November 25, 1883. His remains lie in the cemetery at New Sterling.

Lorenna Evelina and Rev. William B. Pressly had four sons, John McMillen, born July 26, 1859; Samuel Harris, March 21, 1861, and died January 20, 1865, aged four years; William Francis, born January 26, 1864, and Leon Taylor, born March 8, 1870.

John McMillen, eldest child of Lorenna E. and Rev. W. B. Pressly, entered the medical profession. His literary course was in Erskine College, Due West, S. C. He graduated in medicine from the Maryland University. On December 18, 1884, he married Violet Brown, daughter of the late Dr. Brown, of Lincolnton, N. C. He located in Lincolnton, and died there July 2, 1891. His remains lie in the cemetery of that place.

John McMillen and Violet Pressly are the parents of three children, Lola Kate, born January 30, 1887; Josephine, July 21, 1888, and John Mason, April 26, 1890.

William Francis remains with his mother at their home in New Sterling Congregation, Iredell County, N. C. He is a ruling elder in that congregation, Rev. J. C. Boyd, pastor.

Leon Taylor, youngest child of Lorenna E. and Rev. W. B. Pressly was educated in Erskine College, Due West, and is devoting himself to teaching.

Martha Hunter, fifth child of Captain John and Martha Harris, was born on Thursday, March 21, 1799, and was married to Christopher Strong of Chester District, South Carolina, on Thursday evening, March 4, 1824. Christopher Strong was a brother of Rev. Charles Strong, and was born in 1802. Their home was in the bounds of Hopewell, Associate Reformed Church, Chester District, S. C. Christopher died April 9, 1845, aged forty-three years. Martha died April 19, 1855, aged 53. The remains of both lie in the cemetery of Hopewell, S. C.

Their children, six in number, are, Emily, John Harris, who died May 14, 1832, aged one year; Martha Eleanor, Catharine, Mary Letitia and Agnes Caroline.

Emily, first child of Christopher and Martha Strong was born Tuesday, February 28, 1826.

She was married to Thomas Grier Wylie of Chester County, South Carolina, by Rev. Warren Fleniken at the residence of her mother in Chester County, December 23, 1845. They settled in Hickory Grove, York County, S. C., where Thomas Wylie was a successful merchant.

Thomas Grier Wylie died December 27, 1883,

aged seventy-three years. Emily Wylie died March 14, 1885, aged fifty-nine years. Their remains lie in the cemetery at Sharon Associate Reformed Church, York County, S. C. The fruit of this marriage is seven children, John Harris, born February 16, 1848; Martha Mary, August 22, 1850; Margaret Alice, February 23, 1852; Agnes Catharine, September 13, 1855; Ida Belle, August 4, 1857; Laura Davis, March 27, 1861, and Sarah Emily, January 2, 1863.

John Harris, first child of Thomas and Emily Wylie, was married January 11, 1882, to Margaret Isabella Whisonant, daughter of the late Calvin Whisonant, of York County, S. C. These parents have five children: Luncford Grier, born December 22, 1882; Emily Strong, May 18, 1886; Eva Belle, April 17, 1888; Ona Catharine, April 23, 1890, and Mary McDill, July 25, 1892.

Martha Mary, second child of Thomas and Emily Wylie, married John N. McDill, of Chester County, S. C., a merchant located at Hickory Grove, York County, S. C., on March, 1870. J. N. McDill is a ruling elder in Hickory Grove Church. The children of these parents are four: Lula Simonton, born December 31, 1870; Thomas Paul, March 23, 1872; Emma Jeannette, February 6, 1874, and Nixon Moffatt, June 1, 1881.

Lula Simonton, first child of J. N. and Martha Mary McDill, married John K. Allison, son of Dr. J. W. Allison, of York County, S. C., February 1891. They have one child, Harry Clinton, born January 17, 1894. Margaret Alice, third child of Thomas G. and

Emily Wylie, married James Castles, son of the late Dr. Henry Castles, December, 1876.

Agnes Catharine, fourth child of Thomas G. and Emily Wylie, married Thomas M. Whisonant, son of the late Calvin Whisonant, of York County, S. C., April, 1880.

Ida Belle, fifth child, married Henry Leslie, January, 1882. Their children are Rosa Cleo, born March 23, 1884; Thomas Wylie, November 15, 1885; Lois Strong, October 22, 1888, and Mary Belle, November 20, 1892.

Laura Davis, sixth child of Thomas G. and Emily Wylie, married Dr. J. W. Allison, of Hickory Grove, York County, S. C., March, 1889. Their children are Sallie Virginia, born December 17, 1891, and Annie Lyle, October 22, 1893.

Martha Eleanor, third child of Martha H. and Christopher Strong, born March 21, 1830, was married at the home of her parents in Chester County, S. C., August 16, 1848, to William Brice, of Fairfield County, S. C. They removed to Pontotoc County, Mississippi. William Brice was a ruling elder in Bethany Associate Reformed Church for a number of years before his death. He died October 30, 1888, aged eighty-seven years. His remains lie in the cemetery at Bethany Church. These parents have six children, Elizabeth Evelina, Mary Letitia, Kittie Malvina, Martha Emily, Hessie and Christopher Strong.

Elizabeth Evelina, eldest child of Martha E. and William Brice, was born June 24, 1849, and married

W. R. Brice, of Fairfield County, S. C., December 8, 1865. Their home was in Mississippi. Elizabeth Evelina died May 26, 1881, aged thirty-two years. W. R. Brice died August 15, 1886, aged forty years. The following are their children, eight in number: James W., born September 8, 1866, and died July 17, 1879; Samuel Agnew, March 13, 1868; and Boyce Lowry, April 21, 1869, and married Mary Lucas July, 1888. Elizabeth Lorenna, their only child, was born July, 1890.

Ella Lee, fourth child of W. R. and E. E. Brice, was born December 28, 1871, and married W. A. Fort, November 23, 1892. Walter Donald, fifth child, was born October 30, 1873; Dorcas May, October 24, 1875; Madge, June 22, 1877, and Robert, eighth child, born November, 1879, and died December 16, 1880.

Mary Letitia, second child of Martha E. and Wm. Brice, was born August 5, 1851, and married J. S. Parr, of Athens, Ga., May 7, 1874. They have seven children: James Brice, born April 2, 1875; Samaria Letitia, September 19, 1877; Roberta Estelle, April 20, 1880; Mary Eunice, April 24, 1883; Calvin Strong, January 17, 1885; Martha Eleanor, December 23, 1887, and Boyce June 17, 1892.

Kittie Malvina, third child of Martha E. and Wm. Brice, was born November 7, 1854, and married M. B. Reid, of Mississippi, December 23, 1876. They have two children, Chalmers, born July 17, 1878, and Haye, only daughter, born October 20, 1881.

Martha Emily, fourth child of Martha E. and

Wm. Brice, was born April 28, 1856, married J. F. Fitzpatrick March, 1880, and died May 31, 1883, leaving two little girls, Mary Buford, born December 25, 1880, and Emma Estelle, born February 22, 1883.

Hessie, fifth child of Martha E. and Wm. Brice, was born July 20, 1858, and married E. L. Moore, of Marion Junction, Ala., February 8, 1882. The following are their children: Ray, born December 8, 1882; Marvin, August 29, 1884; Eugene Brice, May 7, 1886; Inez, November 4, 1888; Adolphus, February 19, 1891, and Paul, December 6, 1894.

Christopher Strong, sixth child and only son of Martha E. and William Brice, was born April 4, 1864, and married February 22, 1892, Lilla Russell, of Tupelo, Miss. They have one daughter, Mary Eleanor, born June 8, 1894.

Catharine H., fourth child of Martha H. and Christopher Strong, was born in Chester County, S. C., and married Samuel Blair, of York County, S. C., January 11, 1848, at her mother's residence in Chester County, S. C. Five children, the fruit of this marriage, are Mary Agnes, John Christopher; Lowry M., who died December 17, 1882, aged twenty-seven years; Martha Catharine and Ida E. Blair, who died December 2, 1876, aged twenty years.

John Christopher, eldest child of Catharine Harris and Samuel Blair, was married to Margaret P. White, December 10, 1872. She is a native of York County, S. C., but her father having removed to Arkansas, she was married in that state. Their children are seven in number: Elizabeth A., Mary Catharine, William W., Samuel Lowry, Maggie J., deceased; Mason H. and John M.

Mary Agnes, second child of Catharine H. and Samuel Blair, was born in York County, S. C., February 7, 1851. She was married at her father's residence, Blairsville, York County, S. C., by the late Rev. R. A. Ross, D. D., December 17, 1868, to Robert Alexander Patrick, of the same county, son of John R. Patrick, elder in Sharon Associate Reformed Church in York County, but now elder at White Oak, S. C. This young couple removed to White Oak, Fairfield County, S. C., and Robert A. Patrick is a ruling elder in that church. They have eleven children: John Christopher, born September 9, 1870; William Alexander, born September 7, 1872, and died September 18, 1883, aged eleven years; Ida Jeannette, September 15, 1874, and who graduated from the Due West Female College in 1892; Robert Lowry, born January 9, 1877; Agnes Catharine, April 10, 1879; Samuel Mason, March 3, 1881; James Harris, August 24, 1882; Thomas Alexander, November 6, 1883; Sarah Irene, December 7, 1885; Elsie Mabel, born October 2, 1887, and died November 15, 1889, and Paul, March 6, 1890.

Mary Agnes Patrick, mother of these children, died at her home in White Oak, Fairfield County, S. C., after several months of suffering, October 16, 1892. She was laid by the side of her children in the cemetery at White Oak, S. C., who preceded her to the grave.

Martha Catharine fourth child of Catharine H.

and Samuel Blair, born in York County, S. C., was married to W. O. Guy, of Lowrysville, Chester County, S. C., at the residence of her parents, April 8, 1874, by Rev. R. A. Ross, D. D. These parents have nine children, viz.: Florence C., Ida H., Susan A., Lowry J., Maud and Daisy, twins; Essie L., Dora and Clarence O. Their home is in Lowrysville, Chester County, S. C.

Mary Letitia, fifth child of Martha H., and Christopher Strong, was born in Chester County, S. C., 1833. She was married to Samuel J. Wylie of Chester, S. C., January 27, 1850, and died June 2, 1850, aged seventeen years and two months. Her remains lie in the cemetery at Hopewell Church. Samuel J. Wylie's second marriage was to Mary Johnson of Chester County, S. C. He died some years since. His wife survives with seven children. They occupy the well known "Christopher Strong" place—a large brick house, that stands as a monument of former days.

Agnes Caroline, sixth child of Martha Harris and Christopher Strong, was born in Chester County, S. C., November 5, 1837. She was married at her mother's residence August 10, 1853, by Rev. Robert W. Brice to John Brice of Fairfield County, S. C. John Brice died October 21, 1863, aged 62 years. His remains lie in the cemetery at New Hope Church, Fairfield County, S. C. There were only two children by this marriage, Christopher Strong and Johnnie Caroline.

Christopher Strong was born in Fairfield County, S. C., July 16, 1860. He was married to Martha Bell,

September 10, 1884, by Rev. James Boyce, D. D. Martha is a descendant of Hugh Harris, oldest child of John and Eleanor Reynolds Harris, and daughter of Charles E. and Isabella Witherspoon Bell, of Mecklinburgh County, N. C. They have five children, Mark, born July 13, 1886; Agnes Caroline, August 5, 1887; Charles Bell, May 21, 1889; Isabella W., born July 17, 1891, and died October, 1891, and Mary Chalmers, March 10, 1894. Christopher Strong Brice is a ruling elder in New Hope Associate Reformed Church.

Johnnie Caroline, youngest child of Agnes C. and John Brice was born in Fairfield County, S. C., October 18, 1863, only three days before her father's death. She married Rev. John T. Chalmers, and her children are given under his name.

Agnes Caroline Brice, was married the second time to Thomas Patrick Mitchell, of York County, S. C., on February 8, 1866. The marriage took place at her residence in Fairfield County, S. C., the ceremony being performed by Rev. James Boyce, D. D. These parents, Agnes Caroline and Thomas P. Mitchell, have three children, William Foster, Eunice M., and Marion Rebecca, who was born August 28, 1870.

William Foster, eldest child of Agnes C. and Thomas P. Mitchell, was born June 3, 1867. He was partly educated at Erskine College, Due West, S. C., but finished his education in the South Carolina College in 1887. He made choice of the medical profession, and after a full course he graduated from the Maryland

University in 1889. He is now located at Avon, New Hope neighborhood, in the section where he was born and reared, and is meeting with success in his profession.

Eunice M., second child of Agnes C. and Thomas P. Mitchell, was born in Fairfield County, S. C., November 18, 1868. She graduated from the Due West Female College, June 1885, and was married at her father's residence in Fairfield County, S. C., May 8, 1889, to R. George Brice of the same county, son of Calvin Brice, Rev.'s J. T. Chalmers and R. G. Miller officiating. R. G. Brice was born, November 20, 1867, graduated from Erskine College, Due West, in June, 1888, and is a ruling elder in New Hope Associate Reformed Church. Eunice and George Brice have two children, George Wallace, born October 2, 1891 and Olive, born December 16, 1893. The home of this family is at Woodwards, Fairfield County, S. C.

This brings to a close the record of the descendants of Captain John Harris, third son of John and Eleanor Reynolds Harris. We find among the number six who have chosen medicine, and four the law and twelve the ministry as their life work. Of the ministers, C. S. Young, Jas. L. Young and Jno. T. Chalmers are lineal descendants, while Charles Strong, J. C. Chalmers, J. N. Young, J. S. Pressly, J. L. Young, W. B. Pressly, E. P. McClintock, H. M. Henry, and J. E. Johnson are connected by marriage.

If one thing more than another has distinguished

the members of this branch of the Harris family, it is loyalty to the doctrines and principles of the church of the fathers, as a large majority of the descendants, and the ministers without exception, are members of the Associate Reformed Church.

CHAPTER XIII.

JAMES HARRIS, FOURTH AND YOUNGEST SON OF JOHN AND ELEANOR REYNOLDS HARRIS. CONCLUSION.

James Harris, fourth and youngest child of John and Eleanor Reynolds Harris, was born September 1, 1767. He was probably born in Pennsylvania, as his parents left their first settlement in Lancaster County, Pa., to come South in 1767 or 1768.

James remained in the home with his parents, taking care of them in their declining years. Their home was a half mile west of Blackstock Church. A small two-story house occupied a place near the spring. Later, James erected a more commodious dwelling near to the first one, but in convenient distance of the spring, which, by the way, was a model one, being neatly walled with rock, with rock steps leading down to the water, covered with a substantial roof, extending to the indispensable "Spring House" of that day.

Among the early settlers, the house site was largely determined by the location of the spring. A good spring was considered a great blessing, even as far back in history as the settlement of Canaan, for Caleb's daughter, the wife of Othniel, was moved to ask a blessing of her father, "thou hast given me a Southland, give me also springs of water;" "and he gave her the upper springs and the nether springs."

The site of the old home, where the venerable and historic pair spent their last days, is scarcely discernable. The property passed into the hands of Hugh Clark Harris, grandson of John Harris, and all the buildings erected by James were removed years ago to a more elevated location, and are now occupied by Hugh Clark's daughters—Anna Miller and Mason Alexander. As has been stated elsewhere, James was the author of a small work on the subject of Psalmody, published in 1824, called "The Plowman's Letter." Although written by a farmer, as the title indicates, it must have possessed some merit, as persons in the state of Illinois asked and obtained the privilege of issuing another edition, which was done in Oquawka, Ill., in 1854.

At the organization of Blackstock, or Lower Steele Creek Church, James was elected one of the ruling elders, which office he held till his death, which occurred on December 12, 1833, at the age of sixty-six years. He also held the office of civil magistrate for a number of years before his death. James was twice married, first to Nancy Hunter in 1782, sister of his brother John's wife. Nancy died February 28, 1812. The children by this marriage were Eleazer, John Hunter, Mary Selina and Nancy.

Eleazer entered the ministry of the Associate Reformed Presbyterian Synod of the South. We are not informed when and where his college course was taken. He took a full course in the Theological Seminary of the Associate Reformed Church North, in the City of New York, under Rev. John M. Mason, D.D., graduating in 1815. For several years after he entered the ministry, he conducted that popular centre of education, Ebenezer Academy, York District, S. C. He was never a settled pastor, but supplied the vacant churches in the bounds of Synod for a considerable period. Eleazer was thrice married, first in the year 1825, to Jane Kirkpatrick, of Sardis congregation, Mecklinburg County, N. C. She died in the year 1829, during the period he had charge of Ebenezer Academy. She left one child that survived her a few months. Eleazer's second marriage was to Miss Dunn of Alabama. She died in a short time after her marriage, leaving no children.

His third marriage was to Martha Hutchison of Obion County, Tenn. The fruit of this union was seven children. One of his children died at his stepmother's in Steele Creek. The little child had taken sick on the way from Tennessee and was in an exhausted condition when they arrived at the old home, and its death occurred in a few days. In the cemetery of old Blackstock Church a little marble slab bears this inscription, " Eleanor Eve, daughter of Rev. E. Harris, born in Tennessee, December 31, 1837, died in South Carolina November 19, 1838." The remaining six have all passed away. Their names are John Mason, Nancy Naomi, Boston Benoni, Hannah Moore Elizabeth, Martha and "Pet," whose other name could not be ascertained, though his brother-in-law writes, "I never knew his other name, so I called him " Bob," or

"Robert," hence he will be known in this Record as Robert.

Nancy Naomi married, Thornton Guinn. Three children were the fruit of this marriage, William, Alonzo, and Julia. Alonzo is probably the only child of this marriage that survives. He is a resident of Obion County, Tenn. After the death of Thornton Guinn, Nancy married Wm. Frazier. They had one son, name not known. Nancy married a third time but the name of her husband is not given. They had one son, name not known.

Hannah Moore Elizabeth was married to James Bedford of Union City, Tenn., in 1861. She died August, 1879, in the thirty-sixth year of her age. Seven children survive, John Washington, born January 18, 1862; Florence Ann, March, 22, 1863; James, November 23, 1865; Mary, December 3, 1867; Macie, February 11, 1869; A. L., January 2, 1872; and Horace M., September 23, 1876.

Mary Bedford, fourth child of Hannah Moore and James Bedford, married J. T. Johnson of Union City, Tenn.

Robert, the youngest child of Rev. Eleazer and Martha Harris, remained with his mother after his father's death and sustained her until her decease, which took place in 1871. Robert married Miss Fields, removed to Arkansas, his wife died there and he returned to Tennessee with his only child, a daughter. He soon died. His daughter finds a home with her grand parents (Fields) in the state of Missouri.

The latter part of Rev. Eleazer Harris' life was spent in Obion County, Tenn. It is said that he was among the first to preach the Gospel in Troy, Tenn., and organized the Associate Reformed Church there. The exact date of his death has not been ascertained. His remains with those of his wife rest in the Associate Reformed cemetery in Troy, but no marble designates their resting place.

We feel that this record of one the early ministers of the Associate Reformed Church is very incomplete, yet these few facts have been secured after repeated efforts, and we are indebted to the untiring kindness of a disinterested individual for a considerable portion of them.

The writer's personal recollection of Rev. Eleazer Harris is that he was of a melancholy temperament, reserved and unsocial, though sometimes he would indulge in a little wit. On one occasion, when seated at a dinner table surrounded with social relatives, he was asked to carve a tongue. He dished out a delicate slice to each one who, in his estimation, needed a "little more tongue," and to those who needed "no more tongue" he declined serving any. Of course all were expected to enjoy the joke, if it was at the expense of some present. On another occasion we heard him propound a "riddle" to the young people for their amusement. The riddle was on the event of his second marriage to Miss Dunn, and was as follows:

> "Before it begun, it was Dunn,
> When half *done*, it was Dunn,
> And when *done*, it was not Dunn."

John Hunter, second child of James and Nancy Harris, was born in York District, S. C., 1793. He served six months in the war of 1812, married Margaret Hunter August, 1817, daughter of Humphrey Hunter, of Mecklinburg County, N. C., and died December 13, 1832, aged thirty-nine years. Margaret was born in 1799, and died June 1883, aged eighty-four years. Their remains lie in the Blackstock Cemetery. The fruit of this marriage was six children: Nancy Selina, born October 19, 1819, and who passed through the furnace of affliction. In her early school days she was severely attacked with articular rheumatism, which continued with such severity that she was deprived of the use of her limbs, and for twenty years or more before her death was not able to walk. The immediate cause, however, of her death, was a cancerous affection of the throat. She died July, 1861, after a long period of patient suffering, aged forty-one years. The other children are James Hunter, born in York County, S. C., November 5, 1821; Humphrey Amzi, March 4, 1823, and died March 1, 1842; Eleazer Strong, June, 1825, and died February 7, 1844; John Calvin, April, 1827, and Margaret Catharine, August, 1833.

James Hunter, second child of John H. and Margaret Harris, married Louisa Smith, August 30, 1849. Louisa died April, 1867, aged thirty-five years. Her remains lie in Blackstock Cemetery. These parents had six children: Helen Augusta, Jennie Hill, Nannie Rosalia, who died November, 1865; James Watt, who died January, 1853; Margaret Catharine, who died August 30, 1857, and James H., who died April, 1867. Helen Augusta, eldest child of James Hunter and Louisa Harris, was married in York County, S. C., at the home of her father December 12, 1870, to John Epps, of York County, S. C. The children of these parents are the following: Benjamin Drayton, Lou Rosamond, Maggie Grier, Arthur Harris and Pattie Hill.

Jennie Hill, second child of James H. and Louisa Harris, married Joseph Davis December 25, 1883.

James Hunter Harris' second marriage was to Mrs. Lucy (Smith) Grier, widow of John Harris Grier, September 5, 1867. James Calvin and Annie Leigh are the children of this marriage. James Calvin took a course of two years at Stetson University, Deland, Florida. James H. Harris and all of his children reside in Umatilla, Fla.

John Calvin, fifth child of John H. and Margaret Harris, was born April, 1827, and married Martha Smith in 1852. John Calvin was in the Confederate service during the late war, and died in "The Soldier's Home," Raleigh, N. C., September 21, 1894, aged sixty-four. Martha died May 22, 1894. Her remains lie in the Blackstock Cemetery. These parents had six children—Florence Amelia, Joseph Lemuel, Lucy Smith, Maggie Hunter, Willie Bouregard, Nannie Price, Martha John and James Henry. The last two survive. Martha John married Mr. Nance, of North Carolina. They have four children, three sons and a daughter, Martha Elizabeth. James Henry married Miss Rice and settled in Charlotte, N. C.

Margaret Catharine, sixth and youngest child of John H. Harris, was born August, 1833, and married J. Harvey McConnell. Two children were born to these parents, Junius and Charles H., who died August 22, 1856, aged four months. Margaret Catherine died August 10, 1856, aged twenty-two years and eleven months. She and her little son lie in Blackstock Cemetery. J. Harvey McConnell married the second time.

Mary Selina, third child of James and Nancy Harris, married Samuel W. Lindsay, of North Carolina, and died August 25, 1819, in the twenty-third year of her age. Samuel W. Lindsay's second marriage was to Violet McLean, March 16, 1820.

Nancy, fourth child of James and Nancy Harris, died May 11, 1819, age nineteen years. Nancy preceded her sister to the grave three months, and they sleep together in the cemetery at Big Steele Creek.

James Harris' second marriage was to Jane Sloan Hunter, October 28, 1813, daughter of Henry Hunter, Mecklinburg County, N. C. She was born January 11, 1779, and was not related to the first wife. Her stepson, John Hunter Harris, married a niece of hers. Jane Sloan Harris died May 8, 1839, aged sixty years. The children of this marriage are Henry, Robert Harvey and Martha Jane.

Henry, the eldest child of James and Jane S. Harris, was born in York County, S. C., August 25,

1814. He was twice married, first to Jane R. Baldridge, of Bibs County, Tenn., August 28, 1834, daughter of Alexander Baldridge. She was born January 28, 1814, and died April 5, 1844, aged thirty years.

Henry Harris settled in Maury County, Tenn. He removed to that state in March, 1840, and was early elected a ruling elder in the Hopewell Associate Reformed Church of Maury County, Tenn. In that capacity he served the church until his death, which occurred July 9, 1887. His remains lie in the cemetery of Hopewell Church, with wife and children that preceded him to the grave.

Henry Harris was the last one of the grandchildren of John and Eleanor Reynolds Harris that "crossed the river."

In a letter to the writer several years before his death, Henry Harris said: "I have in my possession a large trunk that grandfather brought from Ireland; also two large books printed in 1661, written by Joseph Caryl on the Book of Job. They are quite a curiosity to the present generation, with the long droll way of spelling words, so different from the present time. They have a piece of parchment in them with printing on it, in as good a state of preservation as it ever was."

These are the only articles or relics, so far as we know, that have been handed down to the present generation.

The children of Henry Harris by the first marriage

are Emily Jane, born October 22, 1835; Robert Sylvanus, January 9, 1838, and died September 12, 1838, age nine months; Mary Louisa, born September 1, 1840, and died May 9, 1866, in the twenty-sixth year of her age, and Pamilla Almedia, born December 2, 1843.

Emily Jane, the eldest child of Henry Harris by first marriage, married Nathaniel Peter Wilburn, December 10, 1856. The children of Emily Jane and N. P. Wilburn are Sallie Mason, born September 25, 1857; Carrie Rebecca, born February 10, 1859, and died October 18, 1881, in the twenty-second year of her age; James Henry, August 15, 1860; Nathaniel Wyche, February 27, 1862; Joel Lee, January 12, 1864; Emma Almedia, August 5, 1870; and Mawry Wilburn, born October 7, 1873.

Sallie Mason, eldest child of Emily Jane and N. P. Wilburn, married Joseph Amos Perry, February 24, 1881. Their children are, Clarence Huntly, born November 26, 1881, and Mary Emma, November 10, 1887.

James Henry, third child of Emily Jane and N. P. Wilburn, married Alice Dickerson Philips, June 28, 1883. The fruit of this marriage is one child, James Henry born May 6, 1885. James Henry Wilburn, the father, died August 2, 1885.

Henry Harris' second marriage was to Jane C. Henderson, of Maury County, Tenn., November 27, 1845, who was born January 16, 1815. Jane C. Harris yet survives at the ripe age of eighty years.

The following are the children of this marriage: Euphemia Elizabeth, Martha Maria, James Harvey, born January 3, 1847, and died July 21, 1854, and Sarah Orlena, born February 16, 1857.

Euphemia Elizabeth, eldest child of Henry and Jane C. Harris, was born August 31, 1849. She was married at the home of her parents in Maury County, Tenn., December 15, 1870, to Ransom Green Fleming. The children of these parents are, Edgar Steel, born September 24, 1871, died April 19, 1881; Alfred Harris, February 16, 1873; Katie Brown, November 2, 1874; James Henry, December 24, 1876; Sallie Elma, December 17, 1878; Carrie, March 25, 1882; Houston Green, March 6, 1885; Janie Elizabeth, May 9, 1887, and Willie Albert, March 5, 1889.

Martha Maria, second child of Henry and Jane C. Harris, was born September 11, 1853, and was married at the home of her parents in Maury County, Tenn., to Elijah Coleman Fleming, February 14, 1884. The following are their children: Sallie Ruchelle, born March 21, 1885; Jennie Harris, May 27, 1887; Edward Franklin, November 30, 1889, and Sydney Ramsey, February 22, 1892, and died September 30, 1894.

Robert Harvey, second child of James Harris by second marriage, was born in York County, S. C., March 9, 1816. He, with his mother and an only sister, occupied the home of the venerated grandparents, John and Eleanor Harris, after the death of his father. He was an exemplary youth and bade fair to fill his father's place in the church, but he was cut down in early manhood, and in a few days this happy home was dismantled. He preceded his mother to the grave only two days. Their separation was short. He died May 6, 1839, in the twenty-third year of his age. His mother died May 8, 1839. Their bodies lie in the cemetery at Big Steele Creek. Martha Jane, the only inmate left, found a home with her brother, Henry Harris, in Maury County, Tenn.

Martha Jane, third and youngest child of James Harris by the second marriage, was born in York County, S. C., March 17, 1822. She was married at the residence of her brother Henry Harris, in Maury County, Tenn., November 18, 1841, to Rev. Neil M. Gordon, of the Associate Reformed Church. He was a son of John Gordon, Esq., of Elbert County, Ga., and was born in that county. He graduated from Miami University, Oxford, O., about the year 1838. His theological course was in the Seminary at Due West, and he was licensed and ordained by the Second Presbytery of "The Synod of the South." For some months he supplied Hopewell congregation, in Maury County, Tenn. In 1842, he accepted a call from churches in Jessamine County, Ky., and was installed pastor by the Kentucky Presbytery.

Rev. N. M. and M. J. Gordon had one daughter, Sarah Jane, who died in 1844, aged two years. Martha Jane died November 8, 1845, in the twenty-fourth year of her age, and with her death closed her family record. She and her babe sleep in Kentucky soil.

Later, Rev. Neill M. Gordon married a daughter

of Rev. Smith, D. D., of the General Assembly Presbyterian Church, and after this marriage connected with the General Assembly Presbyterian Church. The surviving children of the second marriage are residents of Kentucky.

This exhausts our fund of information concerning the family of James Harris, fourth and youngest son of John and Eleanor Reynolds Harris. Eleazer Harris and N. M. Gordon are the only ministers connected with this branch, who, with twenty-nine of the Hugh Harris branch, the six of Robert's and twelve of John's, gives a total of forty-nine ministers among the descendants of this pious and honored pair. The promise has been more than fulfilled in their experience:

> "How blest the man that fears the Lord,
> And makes His law his chief delight;
> His seed shall share his great reward,
> And on the earth be men of might."

Conclusion.

Having traced as far as we had reliable information the descendants of Hugh, Robert, John and James Harris, the four sons of John and Eleanor Reynolds Harris, we repeat what was said in the Preface, that our sole regret is that the records of all the branches are not full and complete. But if our efforts shall prove instrumental in perpetuating the memory of our honored ancestors, of introducing and bringing about a more intimate acquaintance among those who are comparative strangers, of fostering a closer and warmer friendship among those in whose veins courses the blood of a common parentage, or of creating a greater interest in our family records and history, we shall feel amply repaid.

We have written, not with a view of fostering the " pride of birth," but that the present generation may feel the stimulus of a high and noble ancestry, for it is a great thing to be able to trace our lineage back to parents, robust and strong, and full of faith in God and His word.

"The claim of birth is buffeted with scorn only when it stands upon the merit of the past which it is powerless to reproduce." But if the blood that courses through the veins of children, and of children's children, bears upon its tide the rich legacy of virtue and piety by which it was first distinguished, then even the "pride of ancestry" is shorn of its offence. It is the impress of character which honorable descendants should be most careful to preserve. It is one thing to be proud of our ancestors. It is another thing to have our children proud of us. As we owe a debt of gratitude to the fathers, the influence of whose character streams into our lives, shedding baptisms and benedictions upon the present generation, so likewise are we under equal obligations to posterity, who are to receive at our hands the rich legacy and sacred trusts bequeathed us by the fathers, and who in turn will pronounce upon our fidelity.

And now it is not without a sentiment of sadness that we lay down our pen and part company with our manuscript, committing it to the tender mercies of a large and generous host of relatives and friends. It has been our companion for weeks, and even months, and in its preparation we feel that we have been in the society of the good and great,—a mighty company,

>   ———" whose foremost ranks
>   Long since had cross'd the river and had pitch'd
>   Their tents upon the everlasting hills."

Many of the living we shall never see in the flesh, but may we not all so love and serve our father's God as not only to receive from loved ones left behind the precious commendation,

> " Life's race well run,
> Life's work well done,
> Life's crown well won",

but also to meet each other in glad and glorious reunion,

> ";Within the mansions of our Father's house,
> A circle never to be sunder'd more,
> No broken link, a family in heaven."

www.ingramcontent.com/pod-product-compliance
Lightning Source LLC
Chambersburg PA
CBHW022114160426
43197CB00009B/1015